This Endless Moment

2nd Edition

Other books by Wayne C. Allen

Available on Amazon as Paperbacks, and as Kindle e-books:

Half Asleep in the Buddha Hall

Wayne's "Eastern" book takes you by the hand and helps you to find peace of mind. *Half Asleep in the Buddha Hall* is a Zen-based guide to living life fully and deeply. Using Zen stories old and new, as well as other illustrations and exercises, Wayne C. Allen takes you on an adventure into the uncharted territory of yourself.

Living Life in Growing Orbits

Living Life in Growing Orbits is a Workbook for people seeking clarity and focus.

In an often confusing world, pure, simple, and focussed guidance is required. *Living Life in Growing Orbits* is a guidebook for discovering who you are. More importantly, it is the tool you need to become fully yourself.

With weekly thoughts and daily meditations and projects, *Living Life in Growing Orbits: 52 Weeks to Wholeness* will help you to change your life.

If you are wondering what to do to learn more about who you are, who you might be, and about your place in the world, this book is for you.

In 52 weeks, you will have found direction and purpose, as you explore the meaning of centred, meaning-filled, and "present" living.

Find Your Perfect Partner

Back in 1999, Wayne wrote a booklet called "The List of 50." "The List" was a guide to deciding whom you want to be in a relationship with, and how to put what you decided into action.

The booklet was expanded into a 100-page book that explains how to *consciously* find your perfect partner. There are comments from readers, as well as sample "Lists of 50." All in all, *Find Your Perfect Partner* is a great way to look for a new partner.

The. Best. Relationship. Ever.

The. Best. Relationship. Ever. is both a learning tool and a step-by-step guide — a plan you will implement — to chart a new direction for your life and relationship.

As you read, you *will* discover:

- 8 reasons you've failed at relating — we examine what goes wrong
- 3 problems people have with communication — once you know what doesn't work, you're ready for what does!
- Sam and Sally, and learn how to really mess up a relationship! — you see their missteps and learn from them.
- a brand new model for being in relationship. I call this Elegant, Intimate Relating.
- how "labelling" your partner gets in the way of Elegant, Intimate Relating. You'll see that Elegant, Intimate Relating means no judging and no blaming.
- the rules and practice of dialogue. Each conversation is worthy of excellent communication!
- what to do, and when. You'll have the tools you need, right in front of you.

This Endless Moment

2nd Edition

Wayne C. Allen, M.Th.

2016

The Phoenix Centre Press
324-55 Northfield Drive East
Waterloo, On N2K3T6

website: http://www.phoenixcentrepress.com

Allen, Wayne Charles, 1951—

This Endless Moment

ISBN: 9780987719294

1. Self-help, health. 2. Self-actualization
3. Mind, body and Spirit

158.1

The Phoenix Centre for Creative Living
324-55 Northfield Drive East
Waterloo, On N2K3T6

Dedication

To Darlene MacNaughton—Darbella continues to amaze and inspire me. I am delighted to spend my life with her and to watch her live her elegant life. I have and continue to give her my heart.

To Ben Wong and Jock McKeen, and to Gloria Taylor, my friends and mentors—who have, over the years, walked with me, laughed with and at me, and continue to re-mind me to be me.

To Ram Dass—I met R.D. only once, at a lecture in Toronto in 1982 (I was the "sound guy!") I am deeply in love with his way of being and the twinkle in his eyes. Studying his thinking has caused me to shift my focus, commitment, and faith understanding.

Dedication

To Darlene MacNaughton—Darbella continues to amaze and inspire me. I am delighted to spend my life with her and to watch her live her elegant life. I have and continue to give her my heart.

To Ben Wong and Jock McKeen, and to Gloria Taylor, my friends and mentors—who have, over the years, walked with me, laughed with and at me, and continue to re-mind me to be me.

To Ram Dass—I met R.D. only once, at a lecture in Toronto in 1982 (I was the "sound guy!") I am deeply in love with his way of being and the twinkle in his eyes. Studying his thinking has caused me to shift my focus, commitment, and faith understanding.

Table of Contents

ACKNOWLEDGEMENTS AND "CAST OF CHARACTERS" I

INTRODUCTION TO THE 2016 EDITION II

ORIGINAL INTRODUCTION III

BEGINNING AT THE BEGINNING

Preliminaries 1

Everything is a figment of your imagination 1

Nothing is happening to you 7

Life just is 11

Get over yourself 13

Have a Breath 15

DECONSTRUCTING THE EGO: AN OVERVIEW

Deconstruction 21

IDEAS AND METAPHORS

Is it working? 35

The Games we Play 36

Wants and Needs 39

You make me feel… 42

If it ain't broke, don't fix it 45

The Poignancy of the Now 47

You exist as a part of others' imaginations 51

Accepting our Emotions 53

Dialogue 57

The Kayak 60

Self-actualized vs. Self-absorbed 62

On Being Self Centred 65

Drama 68

Getting the Joke 71

Waiting for Godot 73

Driving Forces 74

You Can't Have It All — The Perils of Entitlement 76

The Fixer-Upper 80

WAYS INSIDE: EASTERN APPROACHES

The Illusion of a Self 87

What is Being Awake? 91

On Just Sitting 97

On Change and Choice 103

Ceilings and The Dynamics of Depression 106

It Is What It is 111

Self-Responsibility and Waking Up 114

RELATING — PASSION'S POWER

Intimacy and Passion 119

Grasping Loosely and Letting Go 121

Passionate Expression 124

SEX, LOVE, AND THE JOURNEY TO COMPASSION

Sex as Fun 129

Love Helps me to Know my Name 133

Choosing Compassion 136

A Summary 139

ENGAGING AT THE CORE — BODY KNOWING

Making Contact 145

The Sex Gene 148

A Look at Bodily Relating: Effective Affection 151

A Look at Bodily Relating: Sensuality 155

A Look at Bodily Relating: Eroticism & Sexuality 160

The Uses and Abuses of Sex 162

GETTING ON WITH IT

On Pissing Your Life Away 169

Locational Enlightenment 171

Soft Eyes 174

Going Along for the Ride of your Life 178

Mentors along the Way 181

How Will You Choose to Live? **182**

The Silent Centre **183**

ON STAYING AWAKE— THOUGHTS AND SUGGESTIONS

Ideas for living in This Endless Moment **187**
One: It's not the Emotion, It's the Interpretation 187
Two: Create an "Awake Moments" Journal 189
Three: Set a Timer 190
Four: Have a Slow Talk 190
Five: Learn to Juggle 192
Six: Eat With Deliberation 193
Seven: To Get Ahead, Retreat 193
Eight: Four Hands Are Better than None 194
Nine: Picture That 195
Ten: Use Music to Move You 196
Eleven: Dance Like Your Life Depends on It 196
Twelve: Build a Support Team 197
Thirteen: Silence Sounds Good 198
Fourteen: Be Simple Minded 199
Fifteen: I could have peace instead of this 199
Sixteen: Tiger Walking 200
Seventeen: Let Go of Outside, Embrace Inside 201
Eighteen: Find a Symbol 202

NOTES FROM THE EDGE 203

Acknowledgements and "Cast of Characters"

First of all, a word about me, so you'll know "where I'm coming from."

I'm a retired psychotherapist; I began that work in 1981. I worked with clients using a humanistic and transpersonal framework.

My other life focus comes from Zen Buddhism. I see my role much more as a teacher than as a therapist, per se, as my goal is to help clients come up with more elegant ways of living their lives.

My partner in life and in the pleasure of living is Darlene MacNaughton. We've been together since 1983, and my life with Dar is amazing and rich. Before she retired, Darbella taught hearing impaired 7th and 8th graders, and she simply and joyfully lives the principles suggested in this book.

Please note that I use quotes around many words. For instance, "true." I am following the authors of *Language, Structure and Change* here—they write that good constructivists know that what we call "objective reality," "true" or "false," "right" or "wrong," etc. are simply expressions of *personal perspective*. They use the term **'objectivity in brackets'** — and suggest putting such words in brackets to remind us of this. The bibliographic reference to their book appears in the text.

Introduction to the 2016 edition

Hard to believe that it's been 12 years since I started working on this book. I had thought about writing it for a while, and requests kept coming, so I finally got my act together and did it.

The book has done well for itself; it's been used as a textbook, has been purchased globally, and has garnered some nice comments and reviews. My favourite story: I was about to attend a course. I introduced myself to a few people sitting in the lounge, and one guy said, "Are you the guy who wrote *This Endless Moment*?"

I was quite surprised by the 'out of the blue' question. He told me that the book had led him to start down a new path and that he was changing his life.

I can't tell you what a warm feeling I had, as all I'd ever hoped for with this book was that people would read it, think about how they were 'doing and being,' and might find an idea or two about how to shift what was getting in their way.

Several books and multiple years later I'm retired, and Darbella and I are doing a lot of travelling. I still write a weekly blog and wish the same thing: that something I write might touch you, be of benefit, and that you'll be encouraged to try something new.

This version of *This Endless Moment* has several new sections, as well as exercises designed to help you experiment with what you're reading. I've shifted the language in a couple of places, as I've changed my language over the years. Hopefully, the changes will make the book even easier to read.

Do be in contact (waynecallen@phoenixcentre.com) I'd love to hear how the book is for you. And because independent authors need the support only reviews can garner, if you like the book, please return to the online store you bought it from, and leave one!

Original Introduction

A client made a request—that I write a book of essays reminding clients of the salient points of my understanding of living the enlightened life. So, I did!

You'll find ideas and concepts that I find essential to anyone seeking a rich and full life. The ideas are interconnected seeds—the order of the topics in the book is arbitrary rather than sequential. You'll find that ideas circle and loop around. I encourage you to read each thought unto itself, *and* as a part of a larger picture.

Clients come in for therapy because something (or several somethings) isn't working. Yet, on an entirely different level (and the point of this book)—the real issue is not what isn't working. The real issue is that they don't understand that solving their issue requires that they behave ***differently***.

There is an internal battle going on in each of us, between the seductive siren song of staying stuck in the "way I've always done life" and the orderly discipline of doing things in another way.

Most people waste their lives doing everything they can think of to get ***others*** to do things differently. There is a considerable emotional investment in this effort. (Let me be clear about which effort we are talking about: the effort of trying to get **the world** to cooperate in making you happy. Now, "the world" can be a boss, a partner, one's parents or kids, your friends... or even the person serving you a double fat-free latte.)

The first step toward gaining wisdom is to understand that you can't manipulate others or "the world" to make you happy.

In a sense, all that I ever "teach" clients (and all I ever remind myself) is this: I am responsible for me, and I am responsible for how I choose to approach my life. Nothing else is "going on." This is such a simple point that it flies directly over the head of 95% of the population.

You'll discover that I love telling stories. Here's the first:

I watched this misunderstanding (which I suppose you could call the "What Do You Mean **I** Have to Fix **Me**?" game) surface and resurface at a *Zazen* Workshop Dar and I attended a couple of weeks ago. The *Sensei* (teacher) was a bubbly woman, full of the simplicity of a *Zen* focus. In a sense, *Zen* can be reduced to meditation—to *Zazen*,[1] because in the end there is nothing to understand. There is just being fully present in this moment...and this moment... and this moment. (Sort of the point of this book...)

The *Sensei* said *Zen* is not a religion, nor a philosophy nor a therapy. A guy raised his hand. He sighed, deeply. He said, "I am a practising Catholic, a philosopher and a psychotherapist. You're asking me to give up everything I believe." (Well, no, she wasn't.) He expressed his discomfort and sadness over his life, trotted out his belief system, sighed and said, in effect, "Here's what I **know**. It doesn't cut it for me anymore, I find no

---

[1] *Zazen* means to understand the essence of the universe; *za*, to sit without moving, like a mountain. *Zen* is neither a theory nor an idea; it is not an intellectual concept. It is a **practice**: correct sitting. *Zazen* practice brings about an interior revolution: a deep wisdom whose essence is unattainable through logical thought alone.)

satisfaction in it, but I'll be damned if I'll give it up." *Sensei* smiled and said, "Just listen, then just sit and breathe."

Another woman kept trying to add New Age concepts and bells and whistles to the *Zazen*. She wanted candles, she wanted music and waterfalls, and she really wanted visions. Sitting and staring at a wall wasn't chargy enough, she said. Always seeking, never finding. *Sensei* smiled and said, "Your mind is too busy; just sit, stare at the wall and breathe."

It's simple.

The key to figuring yourself out is finding a way to remind yourself "how life is." My plan is to encourage you to examine yourself, to slow down, to shut up and to relax a bit. You'll find ideas for changing your focus, for letting go of the need to be other than whom you are, and especially ideas for letting go of tilting against the world. Much of the drama goes away when I simply settle in for the ride, stay present in the moment and accept responsibility for my drama (or lack of it... sometimes, the more elegant choice.)

There is only one way out. Here it is, in short form:

Everything is a figment of your imagination.
Nothing is happening to you.
Life just is.
Now, get over yourself!
And have a breath!

More on these fundamental ideas on the next few pages!

Please Note!

When I write I always insert the following caveat:

No one hurts us without our cooperation— "the hand on the knife that is stabbing us" is our own. This applies ONLY to non-physical interactions. Physical violence is never OK and is never to be accepted. Emotions, on the other hand, need to be expressed, witnessed and gotten over.

Beginning at the Beginning

Preliminaries

As I said in the Introduction, there are certain understandings or requirements for sorting out what's *really* going on with life. Now, it's clear that most people aren't interested in buying into these requirements, as this would require way, way too much responsibility for one's life. And that's too bad, because without the firm foundation of an underpinning structure, everything in life becomes, in reality, the crapshoot it *appears* to be on the surface.

So, let's assume you are sick of playing at life using rules that don't work. You are reading this book because you are ready to accept responsibility for your life. Let's begin by expanding on each of the "foundational ideas" I listed in the Introduction. Once that is out of the way, we'll look at how to apply these ideas to various aspects of life.

Hang on to your hat—this first idea is a complex one, and 'getting it' is essential to the rest of the book. Have a breath, take your time, and think about what you're about to read!

Everything is a figment of your imagination

I mean exactly what I am saying here, literally and figuratively. Another way of putting this is, "everything is relative."

I got to thinking, the other day, about the use of the word ***phenomenon***. Let's think about that word. Here's one of several possible definitions:

> phenomenon: (plural, phenomena) means simply what has appeared (Greek, *phainomai*, to appear).
> It is used in science to express the visible result of an experiment.

Notice that the idea behind the word is "what we **observe** is simply there."

Even if we play with the second definition, about scientific usage, we get: "We did this experiment, and got this result." Any ***phenomenon*** can be described, but it does *not* have a pre-existing definition or meaning. In other words, the scientist would then have to say, "And here is how we *interpret* the phenomenon we just described."

Within this world are endless events (phenomenon) and every one of them **lacks** a universal meaning. I thus find it ironic that people use the word phenomenon to mean *extraordinary*—saying, "That's phenomenal!" In "truth," they are saying, "Look! Something! Right there!"

Notice what would happen if we understood that the world actually **is** phenomenal—that it is a series of unconnected and non-meaningful events. We would have to admit that a thing is a thing is a thing until we "make meaning" about it. To do this requires a leap in our understanding. The leap is summed up thusly:

The meaning I make about the essentially meaningless is only meaningful to *me*.

You may see where this is leading. Society, to maintain order, *insists* that things have conventional, agreed-upon meanings. We agree to agree about these meanings. It's not that we actually or factually agree, but rather that we agree enough to "get stuff done." For example, 'a red octagon with four letters in white' is a sufficient description of the "phenomenon" that most everyone on the planet recognises as a stop sign. On the other hand, how we interpret the *function* of the thing we agree upon is totally subjective. As my mother-in-law demonstrates on a regular basis, a stop sign, in her world, means "slow down, glance around and roll through." ☺

It gets even more interesting when we move into the realm of the intangible, the emotional, and the relational.

To "get this," you must understand what happens when we accept that "*all* is phenomenal." I begin to recognise, and likely with some discomfort, that I am, and my life is, exactly and precisely (and no more than!) how I ***describe*** it.

When you think about it, all disagreements, fights, wars, are about a dissonance between definitions.

Notice that the word disagree means,
"A conflict of people's opinions or actions or characters."

In other words, we disagree because we do not "make the same meaning." Notice that this definition and the word disagree itself contains no reference to "right" or "wrong"—it simply describes a conflict in meaning. To "get the point," then, I need to understand that my perspective is *mine.* Perception is phenomenal (it simply "is," rather than being "true" or "false.")

No matter how dearly I wish it was otherwise.

I worked with a couple that had spent a couple of days disagreeing. (OK. Fighting.) He'd gone along to a party for her friend's birthday. He didn't like the guest of honour—indeed, he'd quickly decided that she was, in his delicate language, "a slut." He'd observed her and decided that her intent was to flirt with and then pick up men.

So far, so good--he can imagine whatever he wishes regarding the phenomenon we'll call Susie. What he thinks, however, falls under the category of "figment of his imagination." In an elegant relationship where good communication is practised, he would have said to his wife, "In my opinion, I judge that Susie is a slut, and I choose to leave." Where the problem—the dis*agree*ment—began was when he said to his wife, "I can't understand why you like her and can't see what a slut she is. Now, everyone is going to think you are one too!"

The wife bit and began to defend her friend. "She's wonderful, and I like being with her, and you hate *all* my friends!"

Him: "O.K. Go down a list of your friends and I'll tell you whether I hate them."

Can you see where this is going?

This type of disagreeing is typical, and basically insoluble. What could be done? Hire a "slut detector?" Take a poll? Grill Susie regarding her intentions? At the end of the day, all we have here is a *difference of opinion*. The story he's telling himself does not match the story his wife is telling herself. And even more interesting, the stories never will match, even if both ***like*** Susie.

This is so because Susie is a meaningless phenomenon, in any world other than her own.

Huh?

Susie simply *is*. She lives her life, does her thing, acts as she chooses (whether she thinks she's choosing or not) and makes nary a ripple in the puddle of another person on the planet. People see Susie passing, and in her wake, they may choose to *interpret*. They make meaning. They create an internal story, a personal perspective, for the phenomenon *Susie*.

As soon as I forget this concept, and move from having a perspective to needing to be "right," I am toast. The couple I just described soon turned to blackmail: "If you love me, you'd see it my way," which is stupid to the nth degree. I'll **never** see it your way, and whether I love you or not doesn't change that.

In the end, with much coaching, the guy said to his wife, "O.K. I don't like Susie, and I have judgments about the way I perceive her behaviour. I wonder what people will think when they see you with her. I think they'll think you're trying to pick up men. I make myself uncomfortable, and I want to take you away from the situation."

In other words: he desperately wanted her to change *her* behaviour so that *he* could be comfortable, and it took a ton of work to get him to see that his other option was to simply stop expecting her to "fix" things for him.

And yet, many of us go there. We assume that, because we are making ourselves uncomfortable, others "should" care—that others "should" immediately alter their behaviour so that we can let go of hurting ourselves. And, of course, we believe this because, at some point, our whining and carping and the stamping of our little, tiny feet got to be so irksome that some fool gave in to us.

Throughout this book, you'll be endlessly aware that I am attempting to help you to let go of manipulating any perspective other than your own. If you continue to turn your attention from *your* discomfort to the behaviour or thinking of another, you have just wandered far away from any hope of a meaningful and peaceful life.

Instead of this endless journey to meaninglessness and ennui, I suggest self-reflection. And that process begins and ends with understanding how phenomenal life is. If you don't like your perspective, your choices and/or your actions, *shift* them. It's all a figment of your imagination, anyway.

This idea bears another look. Imagine this scene: You're married, and you are quite full of yourself (who else would you be full of?) You look at your partner, and "for his own good," you begin to make "suggestions" (which turn into demands) that he change his way of being. Because you are so "special," you can't understand why he resists. Doesn't he know that changing would make you happy? Doesn't he know that love is all about compromise? Can't he understand how important it is that he acts in such a way as to please you?

Now, if you can take a step back, ask yourself this. If the rule is, "If you love me, you'll change," **how come this rule only applies to your partner, and never to *you*?**

We'll be addressing this issue for the rest of this book. The *only* way out of the misery that is your life is through rigorous adoption of the idea that *life is phenomenal.* People see the world the way they see the world because that's the way they see the world. It's not about you. And even if they are standing right there saying all kinds of provocative things to you, that also has nothing to do with you. The only question is whether you will choose to provoke yourself.

The writers of *Language, Structure and Change* [2] (a difficult but essential book) quote the radical constructivist assertion (made by Maturana) that *"life is a purposeless drift."* This is the essence of life and is similar to the Zen principle of emptiness, which suggests that "things" are empty of meaning.

In *zazen* (meditation) you learn to let go of the need to follow your thoughts. As you let go of meaning making—in the moment of silence that occurs—you are fully present in the moment. In that moment, there is "no-thing" because I am not engaged in mental exercises.

Nothing is "real," nothing is "true," all is *phenomenon.* My meaning is my meaning, and it's unique to me. This holds universally, and especially in the world of relationships.

One more example: Hold your hand out, palm toward you. You see lines and fingerprints. Someone sitting opposite you sees your nails and knuckles. A nurse sees veins into which a needle might be inserted. A tattoo artist sees a canvas. We call the thing (in English) a *hand,* and we give common consent that the thing on the end of your arm is indeed called a hand, but that word only describes its *form.* As to its *nature* or its *function,* it is whatever you perceive and declare it to be.

This idea applies to *everything.* In a sense, nothing means anything, and anything means everything. More simply put, "The only thing I know for sure is what I know, for sure." A corollary is, "Things are as they appear to *me.* They are *equally* and *also* how they appear to others."

Typical situation: "I was talking to her, and she 'gave me the look,' and I knew she was mad so I got angry and stomped off." What we just heard was a description of the "reality" *of the person saying this.* Here's the point. Their reality isn't "true" or "real." It's just the story they told themselves.

---

2 Jay S. Efran, Michael D Lukins & Robert J. Lukins, *Language, Structure and Change*, (New York: W.W. Norton, 1990), 23

Here's another description of what happened. "I was talking *at* her, trying to get her to agree with me. She tightened the muscles around her eyes. I stopped talking, made myself angry, and chose to leave the room."

The latter is equally "true," and may even be a bit more accurate because it eliminates the "guessing about my partner" part. As a therapist, I would say, "Was your goal to anger yourself and leave the room? If that was your goal, you succeeded. If your goal was talking with your wife, your judgements (how he described what he thought he was seeing) got in the way of your goal. The way I see it, you have two options:

1) Try to persuade your wife never to squint up her eyes (or to do anything else that you'll piss yourself off over) or

2) Simply note your perception as it drifts purposelessly by and continue talking."

In other words, (and this is why this is perhaps the most important concept in this book) you have to "get" that things mean what you *pretend* they mean. They have no *intrinsic* meaning. Put colloquially, life happens and we put the spin on it. I don't have to like what is happening, but at the same time I don't have to invest it with meaning (bad, evil, doom, and destruction, whatever.)

Here is an event. What do I choose to do about it?

Nothing is happening to you

Ah, the joys of victimhood. The Cult of Victimhood has reared its ugly head for three plus decades now, and began, legitimately enough, in the Civil Rights Movement. People—indeed entire races and genders—have been disadvantaged in the past—this is without question. Past unfairness needed to be addressed. The downside was the creation of the Bureaucracy of the Perpetual Victim.

One of the biggest problems with bureaucracy is the need to create projects to increase funding. Back in the 80s, I opened a Daycare in a church I was working at. After completing a ton of paperwork, the Ontario government gave us a whack of money to outfit the place. I got a pile of catalogues, and the director of the Daycare and I started comparison-shopping and making a shopping list. In came the Social Worker assigned to us. She said, "What are you doing?" I explained that we were looking for bargains. She replied, "This is March 10. Our fiscal year ends March 31. Just spend the money. I can always get you more, but only if you spend this lot first."

I later discovered that this same rule applied to other areas of Social Work. To keep departmental and project funding from year to year, all the money allotted *had* to be spent. If it wasn't, the budget would decrease for the next year. So, a major task in Social Work was to go out and harvest an endless stream of "victims in need of rescue." If that didn't do it, they'd invent new kinds of victims. New programs were then created to treat the newly created victims.

Of course, the perverse part of this is that many helping professionals get into counselling, or Social Work, the ministry, personal development, etc. because they are pulled to "help." For helpers to help, there needs to be an endless supply of "helpees." The helper is thus co-dependent with the helpee. Until one or the other breaks out of the loop.

Given the addictiveness of helping it is easier for the *victim* to simply grow up and step away from such thinking. Most *helpers*, because their identity is tied up in helping, are loath to end the game.

Similarly, in the "civilian" world, I can't tell you how many people come into therapy and try to co-opt me into "curing" *their partner*. This is related to what we said, above, about perspective and phenomena.

Weirdly, if I see my problem as located *outside* of myself, *and* if I make it my "mission in life" to fix the *other* person, the last thing I want is for them to be "fixed." If they are "fixed," then whom do I blame for what's wrong with my life?

You'll notice that the pattern here is sort of like a dance. It requires two people to tango. If I see myself as a participant in a dance that is happening "to" me, and that, at some level, how I "am" is determined not by me but by my circumstance(s), I am, by definition, helpless. This, of course, works from either side of the dance.

The victim has someone or something to "blame." Doesn't matter what—parents, genetics, past traumas, current dilemmas—so long as I see myself as *non*-responsible, my fate and the outcome is out of my hands.

If I am the *rescuer* of the victim, my happiness is also outside of myself. My purpose—my intention—is to "fix (s)he who is broken." My willingness to do this dance means that I *have to* help, but only to maintain the status quo. This helper mentality can be so strong that if by some miracle, the victim gives up that role, often the rescuer will, at that point, leave the relationship to go find another victim to rescue.

If we move our attention back to the first point, that nothing means anything *intrinsically,* then you begin to understand how subjective blaming is. By the end of this book, if all that you understand is this one point, you'll have figured out what 95% of the population never figures out.

Blame is simply one choice of many.

Let's, for the sake of argument, pretend that someone is doing something that could be understood as attacking behaviour. (Let me hasten to add my favourite caveat. When I say nothing is happening to you, I am *excluding* physical violence.) What someone *says* to me has no innate meaning—it only means what I mean it to mean.

Take the illustration, above, about the guy with the problem around his wife's friend Susie. Now, when he goes into lecture mode, then anger mode, she could respond by sitting there "helplessly" and think she is hard done by. She could think he is attacking her. If she thinks this, she could choose to pull in and clam up, or she could fight back by attempting to hurt him in return.

The choice we're suggesting is this: instead of these useless behaviours, she *also* could choose to understand that he is doing what he is doing, and that her role is to step out of *his* drama and simply be present with him until he gets over himself.

If she shifts in this way, suddenly her choices are *infinite.* This, however, is only possible if she accepts as "true" that no one is doing anything to her. Only *she* can do something to her.

The *Zen Sensei* I mentioned in the Intro has this figured out. When she dealt with the guy who was scaring himself about thinking he'd have to change his beliefs (of course, that is exactly what would be required, should he wish his life to be different) rather than getting caught up in his drama, she simply encouraged him to sit and breathe. My shorthand for this is, "Have a breath and get over yourself."

I suppose the *Sensei* could have taken offence, defended herself, explained herself, or in some other way joined in the drama the man was making for himself. Instead she "allowed" him to be stuck (to stick himself) and invited him to pick another alternative. Let's be clear—the issue was his, no matter how badly he wanted to make it "all about her." There is a world of difference between "You are making me uncomfortable," and "I am choosing to discomfort myself over this."

Another guy at the workshop said, "Do male *Sensei* talk as much as female *Sensei*?" Couched in this seemingly innocuous question is (he later admitted) the discomfort he was feeling over what he *thought* was going to happen at the workshop vs. what was *actually* happening. Again, to assume that the *Sensei* would change so he wouldn't be uncomfortable is silly.

To really 'get' this point, spend some time reminding yourself, experience by experience, that "nothing is happening."

Once you get this, you can add, "All that is happening here is what I choose to believe is happening."

Life just is

Because of our sense of (or wish for) *importance*, we pretend that the things happening around us are *also* important, or significant. Thus, it becomes easy to ask, "Why is this happening to *me*?" I call this entitlement thinking, which is the same as thinking that one deserves special treatment.

Now, you may be thinking, "Right! Of course, I deserve special treatment, because I'm so... well... special!" And you know, you might just be every bit as special as you think you are. However—and here's the catch—as well as the piece you don't want to hear—everyone else is just as special as you are!

Two people are walking along the street and a kid on a bicycle smacks into one of them. Now, the guy who got smacked could be wondering what he did "wrong" to deserve this, why he's "always" getting smacked, why "god" is out to get him, or how come the other guy didn't get smacked. The person who "got missed" might be thinking that "god" must love him, how bad things only happen to bad people so the guy who got smacked must have done something "wrong," or how great it is to live a charmed life. Whatever.

So, would the situation be a "better" story if the roles had been reversed? Better for whom? If something *bad* happens to me, would it have been "better" if it happened to someone else? "No!" I hear you saying. "It would have been better if it hadn't happened to anyone!" O.K. That's nice. I might even agree (although, since I can't see the future, I *don't* agree) but that doesn't change the fact that it *did* happen.

It happened.

It just didn't mean anything.

Why does anything happen to anyone? We don't know. Why the Twin Towers and not the Sears Tower or the Empire

State Building? Why one floor and not another? We don't know. The thing, the scary, strange, thing we refuse to accept is the line from the 60s—shit happens, and then you die.

I'm not trying to be cruel or heartless here. I want you to be free, and that will happen only when you let go of thinking that you should be immune from the crapshoot that is life.

The only thing you have some control over is how you live your life as you deal with *the cards you are dealt.*

Because we love life and because we care about those we like and love, we get into magical thinking, where everything and everyone is "supposed" to cooperate in a "happiness project" where nothing "bad" happens. Lately, I've been saying to clients who think this way, "And what's it like having all those little cartoon bluebirds flitting around you head singing songs, like in a Disney movie?"

If people are as they are and things are as they are, it is difficult to stay stuck in the idea that my wishes, desires and demands are any more significant than the next person's. Of course, they are more important to one person—me! So, the wise soul simply decides to do the best they can with what they want, without the expectation that anyone else (or the world!) is going to put them first.

The corollary to all of this is another interesting idea: "No One is Coming." No matter how much you long to be rescued by the White Knight, it ain't gonna happen. Life happens, and all we get is a choice. Go or stay. Speak or remain silent. Laugh or cry. Dance or feel sorry for yourself. The nice part is, there is always a choice, right up until we die.

My intent is to pique your interest in relating to others and to yourself in a gentle, "purposeless" way—life just is, and I want to share my spin on it with you. In a sense, this book creates a space where we can meet, and where dialogue can take place. To fully engage with life and with others, we must begin by simply acknowledging that life and others are simply *as they are.*

I choose to accept what is in front of me—as it is and in its totality—or I leave.

Respectful living requires that I make no demand that others or the world be other than they are. Instead of tilting at windmills and trying (and failing, always failing) to change the world and others, I simply shift what I can—*my* perception and *my* actions.

Get over yourself

I know. This expression is often used to mean, "You're a pain in the butt and I'm sick of it, so knock it off." Alternatively, it's used to persuade someone to stop having an emotion. The normal usage is to stop another person from doing something you judge to be annoying or painful to *you.*

I mean what I wrote. Your job is to get over *yourself.* As in, pull your attention back to you and to your reactions and responses.

Far too much attention is spent on why *other stuff* must change before *I* can.

Moving past this propensity (and we all have it) to look outside of ourselves for the source of my distress is precisely as difficult as you choose to make it.

As we noted above, our culture has within it a deep belief in victims and blame. We are *externally* focused almost to the exclusion of self-reflective self-responsibility. Shifting things requires a great deal of effort, and sometimes it seems the task is impossible.

Fortunately, brain scientists tell us that there is ¼ of a second between stimulus and response. They further tell us that there is a quicker path to the more ancient and reactive parts of the brain than to the prefrontal cortex (where reasoned, ethical choice happens.) ¼ of a second is not, seemingly, a lot of time to switch from autopilot to choosing a response, but it's more than enough in "brain time," where things are happening at the speed of light.

When we say that enlightenment and happiness is an "inside job," it is reprogramming our understanding regarding choice that we are talking about.

On the other hand, this inside job is *perpetual,* and that's discouraging for most people. The reason it's perpetual is as we just stated. Each thing we perceive goes, virtually simultaneously, to the reactive and to the responsive sections of the brain, and that means that we must choose **each time**. This is what lies behind the Zen-like mantra of "one time and one time and one time." We are never "fixed." There is nothing broken.

There is choiceful behaviour and there is a knee-jerk reaction. You know you are getting over yourself as the frequency of choice over reaction goes up.

I was working with a long-time client recently; she had returned to therapy (grudgingly) after a year or so layoff. She had made great strides, but after the year off was again in pain, both mentally and physically. As she described her situations, all of which ultimately had to do with her reaction to others (she had decided that "people are disrespecting me," and her solution was to pout, distance herself from her partner and make herself sick) I asked her about ***her*** choices.

Boy, did she get angry. First, she went to, "You just don't understand." Then, "People should be treating me better." Then, "Why should *I* have to do all of the work?" Finally, she remembered what we'd talked about in the past, and said, "I forgot that I have to do this *all the time*!"

I just smiled and reminded her of what she knew. She sighed. "I suppose I thought that by now, I shouldn't need to see you. I should be able to do this by myself. And I shouldn't need Bodywork, as I shouldn't be storing stress anymore." I commented on how she had set a record for the number of shoulds in one thought. I reminded her that her only project is to "get over herself, again and again," to have enough sense to check in with someone who is not involved in the drama, and to do this on a regular basis.

I amuse myself at the number of people I know who have done workshops or therapy, and who then assume that they are either "wise" or "fixed" or both. I don't notice any great improvement in their relationships or in the way they choose to torture themselves, but they sure talk a good show.

It would never occur to me to think I "get it," now and forever. I "get it" one time and one time and one time, a lot of the time. And that's as good as it gets. Anytime I think I'm "done," I'm simply fooling myself.

Get over yourself, stop 'should-ing' all over yourself, and go find someone to work with. Stay with it until you die.

Have a Breath

The point of this expression is two-fold. First, it is what it is—a reminder to breathe. Second, it is a tool designed to remind us to slow down, go inside and listen to the voice of our body.

It is so that breathing is something we do indifferently. As a result, our bodies are, in a sense, oxygen starved. Given that oxygen fuels our brains, it's no wonder we get into the messes we get into.

Autopilot

Physiologically, stressors that are of sufficient intensity lead to the "fight or flight" reaction—we tighten our bodies and slow our breathing. There's likely some important reason for this, and when we are under *legitimate* threat, this autopilot reaction is a good thing.

The problem is that many are leading their lives **stuck** on autopilot. We allow ourselves to experience low to mid-level stress pretty much all the time. Ever wary, ever 'antsy,' ever watching our backs, we restlessly wander the planet. The more we sense danger, (and that danger might be "the way my husband looked at me and shook his head") the more we tighten up—fearing attack, we slow our breathing.

The cure, such as it is, is to breathe. The reason Buddhists put so much focus on breath and breathing is that it is an incredibly effective way to bring your attention into the present moment and to calm and centre your body. The other interesting thing that happens as I pull my attention to my breathing, is that I might just shut up for a minute or two and not dig myself deeper into whatever mess I'm creating for myself.

The voice of the body has been called "intuition" or "a gut feeling," or "a heartfelt sense" of what's up. All the parts of the body have a voice, and what they "say" means something. Often the meaning is simple—I'm missing something in my environment (including my interior theatre) and my body wants me to notice it.

I was talking with a new client the other day and I described what I saw regarding the way she carried both herself and her stress. I made a comment in passing about her having put her life on hold for 5 or 6 years, how that seemed to me that she lacked passion, and that passion issues are "pelvic" issues. She said, "I often hurt my lower back or the muscles of my thighs. I thought I just kept picking things up wrong."

Because the connection between body pain and emotional distress is not obvious, I encourage my clients to take their bodies seriously. I don't think that the messages we get from our bodies are "truer" or more important than *head* messages—they're just not *less* important. Intuitive gut feelings are one channel of information, among many. My sense, however, is that this is the channel most people chose to disregard.

I've had clients say, "I feel anxious and out of balance around him, pretty much all the time," as one description of a relationship problem. One woman said, "Mostly, I want to sleep on the other side of the bed. I don't like getting too close to her." Another, "Her voice is like fingers on a chalkboard." This stuff comes out as part of the description of what brings clients into therapy—they're also examples of what they fight about (fight *topics* are transient and pretty much irrelevant.)

When I ask, "Why would you want to stay with someone you don't want to touch?" or "How do you decide to stay with someone when you almost always feel anxiety around him?" I get, "Because I'm committed to the relationship." This makes no sense to me.

And no, I'm not saying we should leave a relationship every time we feel anxious. I *am* asking why we would settle for a relationship in which, for *decades*, my body is screaming, "What in god's name am I doing here?"

Again, I'm not saying that the voice of the body is *primary*. I am saying that it shouldn't be discounted, ignored or disrespected.

Often, this discounting extends to shutting down various aspects of bodily feeling. A common one is to turn off sexually. Another common approach is to eliminate or minimise physical contact: things like hand holding or hugging.

I would go so far as to say that comfort level with and frequency of physical contact is a direct indicator of the health of any relationship.

Healthy relationships are physically expressive relationships. If I am avoiding physical contact with my partner, I am in effect saying, "I refuse to connect with you." The refusal may seem to play out *physically*, but that simply represents what's going on at all the other levels—emotionally, spiritually and in terms of the couple's "couple-ness."

We'll look at this as we go along. For now, let's just think of "have a breath" as a reminder to monitor and deepen our breathing and to slow down enough to be aware of what our body is trying to say. If I am physically drawing away from a situation or a person, it would be very good indeed to explore that choice, as opposed to unreflectively pulling back.

These introductory concepts will be referred to and explored at greater depth in the following sections. What I'm proposing is a fundamental shift in your thinking—one that is required to reach a place of contented, self-responsible living. Please, take your time and think about what you're reading, and then follow through on putting these ideas into practice. You'll be glad you did!

Deconstructing the Ego: an Overview

Deconstruction

I'd like to suggest to you that life is meant to be an ongoing personal development project. This is a concept we accept at work—we "gladly" train and retrain, looking for improvements, efficiencies, other, newer, "better" ways to do things. I suspect we were meant to be on a similar walk in our personal lives, but somehow forgot.

Let me introduce you to a concept I call the ego project. I define the ego project as the societal, tribal "psyche" *working* upon each child—the process of taking the child from an undifferentiated state to having a self, an ego—an individual, individuated personality. This project involves much repression and suppression of parts of ourselves, as we struggle to learn the rules imposed by family and culture.

The ego project, for the clear majority, is complete by early adolescence.

At that stage, the person is just that, a person, standing by herself, alone, unsure, aware of being separate, aware of feeling empty, aware that there is *stuff* that she stuffed. She looks around and sees other people in the same boat, and at some level decides that this is how "adult" life is *supposed* to be. Because she is in discomfort and because she still needs to *physically* differentiate, the average adolescent begins a period of rebellion. She is fighting against "what has been done to her."

Now, **teen rebellion is *not* Deconstruction**—I'll get to Deconstruction in a moment. Teen rebellion is the opposite of childhood *acquiescence.*

As a child, I may be moved, when dad says, "white," to agree, "Yes! White!" No reflection, no evaluation. Teen rebellion is: "No! Green!" This is a *reaction*, not a *response*. It's, "I'll show my independence by acting contrary to my upbringing."

For most people, this is where they stay stuck. For the rest of their life, there is an endless round of conforming, bitching, complaining and rebelling. Thus, most adults in our culture have a "emotional" maturity of a 16-year-old.

Finally, having moved on and/or moved out, adulthood looms. The child to teen to adult cycle is complete; the proto-adult has successfully built an ego structure and is especially aware of the expectations of his/her tribe and culture (T&C).

Here's an example of North American T&C "teachings":

If I am male, I am *expected* to be a breadwinner, to (likely) earn more than any woman I might relate to, and to repress my emotions. If I am a female, I am expected to want both a career and a family, to be able to juggle responsibility without a lot of help from the male in my life, to be nurturing and caring, and to display emotions, but stop if any male in the vicinity becomes uncomfortable. I should never seem aggressive.

And on and on.

Now, at my core, I may be entirely different from the T&C stereotype. I may long to enact a different way of being. But the T&C has done a good job. I have been assured that if I step out of role, I will be banished, possibly killed. If I rock the boat, someone will stop me. I am allowed, *within T&C limits*, to be eccentric, whiny, complaining, and odd—but I believe I will be disowned if I turn my back on the T&C and walk my own path.

I live behind rigid walls. My *body* is tense. My *mind* seems "mushy" around finding another way. My *heart* is not very alive, and I'm neither open nor vulnerable to true intimacy, as I might be *seen*, and therefore abandoned. So I get really good at playing roles and games from behind a solid wall. My *soul* is a vacuum, where I always feel lonely.

As I look around me, I notice that most people simply settle, grudgingly, for this state, as the fear of change, of the unknown, is so *overwhelming*.

If, however, I want to be whole, I recognise that the only way out—the only alternative—is to *challenge each and every belief and each and every wall I ever built up.*

I call this the ***De*construction Project**.

If I am wise, I realise that my goal must be to maintain just enough of the T&C structure to be a functional member of my society. At the same time, I choose to live out a highly expanded version of myself.

Deconstruction is seldom about little things. Typically, the issues confronted are *huge*.

My personal walk through this minefield is illustrative; so let me tell you a couple of stories.

A major deconstruction moment began in my first year of training to be a therapist. My pissy, arrogant personality was celebrated by my supervisor, who gleefully used me to criticize the work of the other interns. I loved the adrenaline rush I got from taking someone apart.

In my second year, Gloria Taylor inherited me and spent a year asking me questions designed to open to me the possibility that I could *choose* other ways of being. Deconstruction of my belief about how I fit in began with my refusing to play the pissy critic. While I cheerfully admit that stopping myself from playing that role was one of the most difficult things I've ever done (a three-year project), I discovered that while changing my essential nature was impossible, repeatedly choosing how to live, act and be was *definitely* possible.

The next year, 1983, out of *fear* that I could not support myself as a therapist, I caved in to the T&C and got a "real" job—I cashed in on my ministry degree and took a church. This did not go well.

I hated almost all of it, except for the preaching and counselling. (Big surprise—Wayne gets off on talking...) I lasted until 1987 and then quit. Started renovating a hotel, while counselling part time. When the renovation project ended, I panicked and took another church. Another crossroads.

I stayed until 1996. I had agreed to be there 7 years (thus, 1994,) but as that deadline approached, I once again doubted I could make it financially. My T&C belief was that "*real* men get a paycheque." And beneath that was the abject terror of stepping outside of the box—of being myself. I thought I would die without my walls and my titles—my roles.

In March of '96, I had a physical breakdown. I thought I was dying, and indeed I was. I was 45, I was spending most of my time doing what I hated, I was a "typical male" in that I overworked and had little time for myself or for Darbella, and I was decidedly caught in living in the future of "someday all of this will be better." I raced back to Gloria, and she suggested I go to The Haven[3] for Phase I.

15 days into the 25-day program, I saw that my life was a house of cards. While I certainly was more "out there" and less bound by convention than most, I had a deadly fear of taking full responsibility for my life and my choices. On fateful day 15, I damaged both of my knees in one hour. I remember standing stock still after the second knee *went* and thinking 2 things: "How do you limp on both legs?" and "I really haven't a leg to stand on."

That "no leg to stand on" line was my entry into *real* Deconstruction. In that moment, I realised that *I had been living a lie*, living a life I had been **programmed** to live—I had been running on **autopilot** while at the same time experiencing

---

[3] **The Haven** - an internationally acclaimed personal development and professional training centre. The Haven offers a wide variety of experientially based courses devoted to the understanding and acceptance of the self and others, blending eastern and western ideas. Thousands have taken courses there and made significant shifts in body/mind/spirit integration and fulfillment of life.

snatches of what freedom, deep relationship and the risk of exercising free will might lead to. I determined to leave the church, and reformulate my being, tearing down that which did not work, building anew on what did.

But when day 25 arrived, and it was time to go home, I regressed. I scared myself about leaving my job, so I decided all I had was a scheduling problem. I'd stay in the church two more years, save up money, and leave *later.* Always later.

I was *dead scared* of taking a leap into the unknown. Rather than explore this, I went into avoidance mode, while distracting myself by becoming hyper-critical of all the people around me. *My arrogance knew no bounds.* To this day, I'm not sure why Dar stuck around for the two weeks it took me to get over myself.

I wanted to be the poster boy for change, the star Haven student and wanted to have this without changing anything *meaningful.* So, the cosmos changed things *for* me.

The son of an elder (whom I stayed with for a day after Phase 1 ended) having heard me describe my Haven experience, flew to Ontario and announced, breathlessly, that I had joined a cult, and that the women, children and small animals of the congregation were no longer safe around me. And amazingly, the elders bought it—hook, line, and sinker. Three weeks after Phase I, I was effectively out of the church, severance package in hand.

Back I flew to Gloria. I have always been good at listening to her and to people (like Darbella) whom I respect. I assume that when something huge happens, my perspective is going to get **caught** in defensiveness, wishing to be special, wishing to have it easy. I'll get whiny and lose the ability to see my choices. So, I immediately talk with those I trust.

Gloria reminded me of why I had gone to The Haven. I had gone there to open myself to the possibility of living my life *differently.* I knew, with my head, that this was possible—I just hadn't thought clearly about how **life-threateningly scary** that change would be. I assumed I could shift a couple of things around (sort of like repositioning the deck chairs on the Titanic...) and that would be that. It never occurred to me (or it did and I dismissed it) that my fear was *justified*. I was about to remove everything I had held to be necessary, as I searched for a new sense of my "real," essential nature.

I was clinging to my security blanket of identity, ("The Minister!") and this "false" identity needed to go away. Because of the strength of my **ego**, it wasn't enough just to leave the ministry. I needed, I guess, to set things up so that my credibility as a minister was in shambles, so I wouldn't be tempted, when scared, to go running back there.

So, there I was, jobless, and I needed to immediately take my part-time counselling work to full time. Well, "immediately" is still going on, *years* later. Funny.

The issue for me was the *gnawing fear of the unknown*—if I followed my heart and Decontructed, who would I be? Would I have friends? Would I die? What if I was completely shunned? And why oh why was this crap happening to me, anyway?

At this point, Gloria proposed the next phase of Deconstruction—*giving up needing to know*.

Ouch. Jeez. I have two Masters' degrees, and I'd always prided myself on my wisdom and intelligence. Not know! What would people think? Who would I be without my swelled head? Without my arrogance? Without my pride? But I trust Gloria, and also love a challenge, so I went for it, heart in my mouth.

Decades later, I still don't know. And that's fine with me.

I still get caught in the occasional drama, but I sense completion of this round of my Deconstruction project. I know who I am and what I am capable of, and as important, what I'm NOT capable of. I understand that I have both integrity and inner and outer consistency. I am living a lot of the time in a state of excited, detached awareness.

When you do the Phase I program at The Haven, they spend 3 days at the end talking about "re-entry." Away from an environment where everyone is involved in this process, entering back into the "real" world, we are confronted with the **resistance** of the world. We may even begin to question the "truth" of what we've started.

Just like I initially did. I thought I could just shift some stuff around and sneak up on change. I feared whom I would become and how I would be perceived. I wondered how to integrate what I was learning into the "real" world. I tried to slow down the process, to understand. Ultimately, I needed to let go, to engage fully in what I was doing. I had to let go of my need to know, to control. I could then begin the process of tearing down and removing all the "stuff" that had been stuffed into me—and my walls came tumbling down.

Yet, it's far easier to stay stuck and to bemoan our fate.
It's far easier to choose to fail,
to patch the walls from the inside,
to push people away, to refuse to listen to mentors,
friends who are also on this path.

Deconstruction requires that we choose to *risk*—facing our fears, owning them, and choosing to go through them, while not knowing where we are or who we are becoming. This is as scary, as dark and deadly as life can get. Mystics call it the Dark Night of the Soul. We are, after all, deconstructing our entire identity, with no plan in hand for what will replace the rotting, no longer safe-for-occupation edifice of our ego.

If we continue, in any way, to cling to our resistance,
we will stay stuck for a long, long time.

As another example of "different yet the same," here's Dar's account of one of her Deconstruction moments—which occurred at a Bodywork workshop I was running. Dar wrote this description to a friend from her "Come Alive" at The Haven:

A friend was at Phase 1 during the month of September. I was away for the month before that. It seems like a long time since we connected. Wayne was out at Haven and had a connection with her. They always do connect at a different level than I do. I hold myself back—fear of rejection and all. I got myself into quite a place of feeling left out and alone. I described it to her as feeling like an attachment—a tag along.

I felt very stuck. I can see now that I was refusing to budge from there. I got quite into blame and expectations of others to make things right for me—if they would only behave the right way and see what I need. Kind of surprised myself how much I got into blame and pointing the finger. Didn't think I did that. Not much chance of getting what I want when I take that tactic.

My friend is having quite the re-entry process from the Phase 1 experience. Wayne's re-entry was quite traumatic but in a very different way. Lots of things happened for him—the shit hit the fan so to speak. My friend seems really stuck. Wayne never appeared stuck but it sure changed his life. Changed mine too.

We spent an evening visiting my friend last week. It raised quite a few issues for me but I worked through those with Wayne. It also raised issues for Wayne and he went through quite the process as well. We have a hot tub and it is great for intense life conversations. Lately, some of our conversations are lasting longer than we can in the hot tub. It is during these times, as we struggle through some difficult stuff together, that our relationship moves to a deeper level.

Yesterday at the workshop I had Bodywork from a couple of people. I was working with people who were new to this. I decided that I would not just go with whatever they were able to figure out. I stopped them a couple of times and let people know what it was that I needed. I've done enough Bodywork to know where my triggers are. I kept my "jaw points" a secret, though. I had more of a voice in this workshop than in any of Wayne's previous workshops. I was pleased about that.

The effects of the Come Alive learnings were still there. It was also a neat energy experience. On the first day of the workshop, I accessed some anger but felt like I was just touching the surface and backing away. Kept giving myself grief over this. I also had it in my head that I needed to cry but the tears would not come. I came away from the experience totally discounting what I had accomplished and the anger that I had expressed because I judged that the anger was not strong enough and I didn't cry. Quite an old pattern for me. **Keep focusing on the things you can't do so you can continue to feel bad about yourself and in this case stuck.** My filters block out totally the things that would allow me to feel good about myself. I wasn't done feeling bad.

One woman had a Haven-like experience. She went right into her emotion and lost control. This was a new experience for her. The others in the group were quite new to the whole concept. Seeing the transformation in her when she returned for the second day reminded me of other people's experiences at Haven and my experience at Haven. At that moment, I remembered my learning from the Come Alive. It is all about **my choice and how I see myself.** I made an immediate switch.

It felt like I flipped a switch. I feel great now. The Bodywork the second day was quite similar to the first day. Got a little closer to the emotion but still didn't cry but that was OK because I was able to get out of my way and have my experience. I also noticed how free I felt to speak out and that helped too. It is amazing what you notice when you lift the filters.

During the last Bodywork session, I had an amazing energy experience. I decided that I was not going any further with the anger and I didn't really want to be pushed on anymore. I directed the person to hold me in the heart area with one hand over my heart and one hand behind my back. I felt incredible warmth and the energy flowed quite freely. After a while, I directed the person to put his hands on my belly just below the navel and one hand on my lower back. (Second Chakra point.) The heat I felt was very intense. After a while, I felt his hand vibrating. At first, I thought it was his attempt to stimulate my energy flow and it was working. The fire in my belly swelled and moved up my spine in a dramatic way. As the experience continued I realised that it was me vibrating—he was vibrating in response to me. It was wild.

At the end I asked him if it was me or him—he did not know but I did—it was me. Kind of nice to feel in a position of directing an experience to achieve what I wanted.

Another interesting aspect of this workshop was a friend of mine from school was there. I had intended on having her over to visit while Wayne was away but her grandmother died and she spent the week in Nova Scotia. She told me she was thinking of coming to the workshop so Wayne came to school and put the pitch on. She decided to come.

I've never really gotten into these experiences much at school. My tendency was to keep things separate. I was both looking forward to and anxious about her being there and my two worlds (my choice!) meeting at the same time. That part of the workshop went well and Carol and I connected in a different way. It will be interesting to bump into someone at school who knows more about me. In general, I tend to be somewhat of a mystery or invisible. Can still do that with some people but in general, I judge that they are not worth my effort.

Darbella describes choosing to step past her blockages and resistance. This continual recognition of and choosing to move through Deconstruction *resistance* is key to the project of the self-responsible dismantling of the walls.

To conclude this section, let me talk about intimate relationships. Why? Because this work is impossible without them. By intimate, I mean open and revealing and present relationships, not necessarily sensual or sexual intimacy, although that's possible too.

I choose to be deeply in relationship with a small circle of friends. With them, I can open myself to my own process, and be open and available to theirs. This process is like being in a strange place with no map—and being grateful for the company. As a matter of fact, the only way through this territory is through trust, not knowledge.

I admit that I am still following the dictate to not understand—to not have answers. My ego wants to scream that I *always* know what I am doing. And my soul laughs, because my soul has no need to know anything. My soul seeks contact, at the boundary, to learn, to play, to dance, to join. I don't know who I am, why I'm choosing to be in the act of relating, nor do I have any agenda or sense of where things are going. I simply choose, again and again, to engage in a relationship, to be present, warm, loving and open. For me, that is enough. My choice. With fear and trembling. And with the assurance that the approval of the world is no longer required. In this is New Being.

Ideas and Metaphors

We begin an exploration of the background concepts that frame a self-responsible world-view. Take your time with all of this, and see how each of the concepts fit for you.

Is it working?

This might be a mechanistic question, but the only real test of the validity of your life is that you are seeing measurable, "positive" results. I'm sure that as you make your way through this book you'll want to divert your attention away from this principle, and you'll be good at it. After all, you've been making excuses for your stuck-ness for years—decades—and doing your life differently requires effort.

For most people, behavioural change comes easily, *except for their blind spot(s.)* When it comes to that place, it's as if a giant vacuum is sucking choice out of their left ear. Instead of a calm discussion of choices and options, the person has a meltdown—and the excuses start. All excuses are one form or another of a few themes— "I couldn't help myself," "(S)he made me do it," "(S)he doesn't love (respect) me," or "It's not fair!!!"

I'm working with a guy who tells me that his goal is to have a strong and positive relationship. Yet, rather than talking with his wife, he lectures. Endlessly. I ask him what he wants. "I want her to listen to me!" he says, with intensity. Well, no. He doesn't. He wants her to *obey* him—to turn to him and say, "Yes darling! You're right! As usual! I've been such a fool, and I'll change immediately!"

Now, in their 10 years together, he's never heard her say that, not even once. Still, he tries. He lectures, he turns red, and he pouts. She turns away.

He *never* gets what he wants most—control. (We can tell that this is his real goal by watching what he is actually doing.) Nor is he getting her to listen; she turns away and tunes him out.

But here's the clincher—he **also** is not getting what he *says* he wants—this would be the "strong and positive relationship" part. From this we can conclude several things—either his definition of "strong and positive relationship" is "one in which I control my partner," or he's lying about wanting a "strong and positive relationship," or he thinks he can get what he wants without having to change anything he's *doing.*

To which we ask, "How's that working for you?"

The only way anything in your life will ever change is by doing something *differently.* Now, admittedly, when you shift your behaviour the behaviour of those around you will also (likely) shift. But that's hardly the point.

***Things* shift when you shift *your* behaviour.**

Waiting for "life" or others to care about the endless whine escaping from your lips and then expecting "life" or others to run around making things better for you just isn't going to happen. In a sense, you need to learn to wholeheartedly engage in the ruthless pursuit of the only "truth" of life—your life is your own, so what's happening to you is about what you're doing and thinking and especially how you're acting. The only test of this is an intensely personal look at whether you are content with your life, your direction, your process and your relationships.

In the end, my client can control only one thing—himself. If he wants a good relationship, he can behave as if he has one. He can drop the lectures, listen to his wife, and share with her what he knows about himself. And if that's not the kind of relationship his wife wants, he can leave.

The Games we Play

In the last section, I briefly mentioned several flavours of excuses. I want to be clear here—the only valid excuse is the one you see in war movies: "Sir! No excuse, sir!"

But oh, how we try!

We blame our parents, our genetics, our race, religion (or lack thereof), society, or the location of the planets or the time of the month. We want someone or something to take pity on us and to make it all better. We whine that we are incapable of doing things differently—and thereby become helpless victims of our favourite excuse.

We imagine that it is someone else's job to "make it all better." It's almost as if we expect that "god," the universe and the people we are in a relationship with should have nothing better to do than to nudge all the elements of life into a row—and "coincidentally" it's the row we want things in.

It's obvious where such faulty thinking comes from—when we were small, our parents likely tried to "make it all better" for us, even right down to kissing our boo-boos and telling us, "All better!" We've been looking for that magic kiss, those magic words, for rescue, ever since.

Problem is, we're not little kids anymore.

Or are you?

God, the number of children in adult bodies that cross my threshold. They wander in, clothes rumpled, looking sad and hard-done-by. They describe their plight. They are being treated unfairly and no one is saving them, or they are knights-errant looking for someone to rescue.

One guy I know is in his third major relationship in 10 years. In each case, he's chosen a woman who was "mistreated by a man!" in her past. Each woman has chosen this man to be her knight in shining armour. In he rides, tells her what to do, and expects gratitude. Gets it. Does it again. Eventually, notices the gratitude is grudging and she's beginning to complain. He's caught on the horns of a dilemma. He wants the woman to "get better" (he wants to fix her) but he *also* wants her to stay defective so he can continue to rescue her.

Eventually, he can't stand the woman and she can't stand

him. So, get this—*he finds another woman and tries the game again*!

The “little kid” part of this guy is this: he has so far refused to take any responsibility for his dysfunctional relationships. He tells me he simply hasn’t found the right woman yet—one who is endlessly screwed up, who takes his rescue and fixes herself, and who nonetheless remains sufficiently needy as to be unable to live without him. Impossible to have, of course, but that hasn’t stopped him. When pressed, he says, “People just don’t understand me!” When pressed further, “But if there were no problems, what would I do? No one would need me!”

Now, of course, the difficulty with being a fixer is that there must be something to fix. So, his other job is to endlessly generate problems, messes, and challenges to fix. And he says, “It’s not my fault! It’s just the way I am!” Well, no. It’s the way he sets it up.

Often, we are blind both to our excuses and to our responsibility for the mess(es) we are in. One of the things a therapist can do for you, if you let him or her, is to provide you with feedback regarding the games you are playing. All of us need someone to talk to who is impartial and honest.

If all you ever do is listen to **yourself**, all you’ll hear is you letting yourself off the hook. Any time you refuse to take responsibility for the mess you’re in, that’s an excuse. One woman put it, “Maybe someday I’ll be ready to take responsibility for my past, present and future.”

I replied, “I don’t think there’s an option.”

You are responsible for where you are today, and that’s all there is to it. On the other hand, you are *not* responsible for what others blame you for. If you’ve been an ass, you can apologise. You can’t take it back, and you can’t do anything to get the other person to stop hurting him or herself. Having said that, your goal is to notice your behaviour, ask yourself the “utility question” (“Is it working?”) and stop making excuses for what doesn’t work.

In the end, the way to stop what isn't working is to stop *doing* what isn't working, preferably with a minimum of blaming, excuse making or whining.

Wants and Needs

So, here's how I define these:

A **want** is something that I value enough to obtain, and for which I am willing to "pay" a fair price.

A **need** is something I think only another person can give me—I expect or demand to be given it **without** having to "pay" for it.

I'll admit my definitions are arbitrary; I mostly want to convey that the two things are *different*. I acknowledge that the two terms are used interchangeably, and in my opinion, "shouldn't" be.

An excellent goal for life is to fulfil wants while minimising needing things from others.

It's not a coincidence that we have a word "needy," but not a word "wanty." It's also not a coincidence that it's hard to come up with a "positive" use of the word needy.

When a client says to me, "He never takes my needs into consideration," it always means, "We're battling over who is the neediest, and I'll be damned if I'm going to lose and give in to him."

Yikes! Who'd want to win that contest???

Apparently, a lot of people.

Example: "I want a back rub" and "I need a back rub" are two different things. If I want it, I can ask, and if the person says (for whatever reason) "no," then I can get it elsewhere. A want, then, might be regarded as a simple transaction, devoid of pressure, emotion or meaning.

If I **need** a back rub, ("Oh! God! Do I ever, really, really, really NEED a back rub!") there is an implied or direct connection between my *need* and my *value* (determined by the response) to the person I need it from. I am valuable (loved) if they meet my need, worthless (unloved) if they refuse. In the world of neediness, a back rub is not a back rub. It's a test.

Being needy—asking or demanding from a position of need—is a sure recipe for relationship disaster. It gets so weird that I have a client who regularly says to his partner, "I need you to want me." Talk about an impossible situation.

Let me go a bit deeper into what I've just written:

Need/want is an illustration of outer/inner confusion. What I've discovered over the years is that I can have pretty much anything I want, so long as I am willing to pay the price and ask around. Thus, a want is mostly internal or "I" focused—I want it, and I can get it. My ego is not involved in what another person chooses to *do* with my want.

Making a demand from neediness is always about *external* validation and power struggle. My ego is directly involved in whether another person puts me first, builds me up, and "makes me feel special." Used as I am suggesting, neediness is about the *expectation* of *external* validation—that others **should** put you (and your needs, because you are needy!) first. You make your plea, and then, anxiously, wait to find out if you are valuable. If you get what you need, you are important to (valued, loved by) the other. If they refuse to fulfil your need, you see yourself as worthless (valueless, unloved.)

Or you decide that they are cruel and heartless.

Even if the "need/needy" word isn't uttered, anytime I think that the person I am relating to should put me first (emphasis on "should,") I'm setting up a "prove my worth to me" situation. Now, this is not to say that my partner would *never* put my wants ahead of hers; it is to say that this decision would be her *choice*, not an obligation.

Only highly insecure, frightened people are needy. Being needy happens to all of us, but if neediness is a lifestyle choice for you, run, don't walk, to a competent therapist.

Now, I know that all this flies in the face of what most people think "love" is all about: the "If it's 'true' love (s)he'll move heaven and earth to make me happy" crapola. People in dysfunctional relationships often say, "If you love me, you'll do it my way."

This is a truly stupid idea. It's stupid because it **demands** that your partner make it his/her never-ending job to do what you want them to. They cease to be human—to have wants, desires and opinions of their own—it's not their job to do anything other than to reinforce your worth through obedience to your neediness.

When a client utters these words, I encourage their partner to reply, "And if **you** love ***me***, you'll do it **my** way!" and then burst out laughing.

Nonetheless, many people think that love means always being coddled, adored, and obeyed. Again, it goes back to that time when we were small and helpless and the centre of our parents' attention. The little kid in us **needs** to be the centre of the universe. And, oddly, ("How dare (s)he!") our partner may be thinking the same.

The way out of this dilemma is to remind yourself that you are the centre of **your own** universe, **and no one else's**. You have every right to have a ton of wants, and to go after the ones you *really* want. What you want to let go of is thinking you have some "right" to demand that someone else endlessly fulfill your needs.

On the other hand, one characteristic of an authentic, meaningful relationship is that both parties willingly **choose** to honour each other's requests (wants). If I am in a highly functioning relationship, 90-95% of my requests (wants) will be honoured **and vice versa.** After all, why would I choose to hang around with someone who only wants to say "no?"

Here is my perspective: I *choose* to spend my life with Darbella, and I *need* nothing from her. I **want** to be with her—openly, honestly, and with vulnerability. I just don't **need** to be, nor is there anything she **must** do for me so that I won't just melt away into a little puddle of insecurity. Our relationship is a choiceful meeting of equals, not a power trip or a manipulative game.

If you insist on being needy, please, go off somewhere and do it by yourself. Give the rest of us a break.

And here's a flash: if you are surrounded by needy people who call or drop in and demand that you look after them, go have a look in the mirror and decide why you are so needy yourself. You set it up. You *need* to be needed. Give yourself a shake, and get a new group of friends.

You make me feel…

Well, no, you don't, although it can seem that way.

A client recently said to her partner, "I feel like less of a woman when you look at other women." A male client said, "I feel like more of a man when people treat me with deference and respect." Another client said, "I feel that I need a man to validate me..." (Being me, hearing the last one generated an image of a man stuffing her into a toll booth for a parking validation stamp on her forehead.)

I want to be able to empathise with my clients, so I've tried to figure out what feeling like less of a man (since I am one) would feel like, and how this would happen because of something external to me. I can't do it. As hard as I try, I can't see myself or my clients as less than we are.

My masculinity is part of who I am, this time around. I can choose to see myself as a hippopotamus if I want to, but it doesn't make me one. I am always and only who I am, and that has nothing to do with things or people outside of me.

I have never seen a case where someone has *made* someone *feel* something.

Some time ago there was a truck commercial running in Canada with a guy singing along to Shania Twain's "Man, I feel Like a Woman." The other guys in the truck are making themselves uncomfortable (it's the point of the commercial—only weird behaviour could make you uncomfortable in this truck) listening to him. But we get the joke. *Singing* that he feels like a woman doesn't mean anything, other than that he is quite strange. And as for Shania, what else would she feel like?

The cure, such as it is, for "make me feel-isms" is changing the language to, "I'm choosing to feel..." Even better, drop the word "feel" altogether, and make it, "Man, I **Think** I'm a Woman..." or whatever. This change of emphasis reminds me that I oversee how I think and how I interpret what I feel.

I'm even entitled to think dumb stuff. If I want to think I am incomplete, I am free to do so. I can also believe that others make me into something other than who I am. It's just not true... or even overly sensible to do so.

The "validation" person, above, is a perfect example of someone who has her life on hold, as she waits for permission to be who she already is. Isn't it odd that we think like this: I do this, and I do this well, and I'll know that I did this and did it well when **someone else** tells me. In a sense, we declare "what is" to be "not real" until it's blessed by the approval of another.

Do I occasionally **need** to hear Dar say, "Boy! Are you terrific!" Yes, of course, I do. On the other hand, I know that this is a ***need***, and therefore a somewhat silly remnant of my immaturity. So, I turn to Dar and say, "I really need to hear you say 'Boy! Are you terrific!' Would you please say that for me?"

She grins, says, "Sure!" and feeds me the line in a sing-song-y, mommy's voice. Amazingly, I make myself "feel" better as she performs this little act. However, I'm always conscious of what I am asking for, and how immature the request is. We make a game out of it, and it's over quickly.

On the other hand, if I'm sad or lonely or wanting some contact, I can ask for a hug or a shoulder and some support, and this too is provided. And vice versa. In this case, I am expressing a want that might **also** be a need. What differentiates it from the stuff in the last section is that I am not trying to manipulate Dar into looking after me, nor am I making a request for a hug or a shoulder into anything beyond a hug or a shoulder. She then can choose to provide what I requested, in a clean, clear and supportive way. She recognises that she is providing the shoulder, and I am providing the "getting over myself" as I rest upon her shoulder.

In an elegant relationship, what you provide to your partner is honesty, openness, a witness to their life, and physical contact. What you do not provide are answers, solutions, fixes, manipulations or healing. Healing, feelings and meaning are always an inside job.

It's hard to let go of the idea that love is about completing another or that love equals rescue. Sometimes, most times, the loving act is to "sit with" someone and in that way to be present with their pain or drama. Sometimes the loving act is to let the person sit alone, giving them space. Never is the loving act to rush in and mess around with someone else's life. (If you absolutely must, limit yourself to making them a casserole.)

Be a witness to what you feel, what you think and what you create. Be a witness (and a support when asked) to the feelings, thoughts and dramas of those you love. This is enough.

If it ain't broke, don't fix it

Broken thinking is this: there is something wrong with all of us. Therefore, the goal of life is to fix what is broken.

We think it, but it isn't "true." In most regards, we're fine the way we are. As you may have gathered by reading this far, I want you to accept yourself, warts and all, and then work hard at making better choices. In other words, you ain't broken and there's nothing to fix.

And this applies to everyone else, too!

My style of therapy is additive rather than subtractive. The last thing I want to do is to help people be even less than they are already choosing to be. The world suffers because people think they have nothing to offer. What I want people to learn is that, far from being one note, option-less people, what they are is stuck in a rut. In a sense, I remind clients of what they already know—of other approaches, often unused, of ways to do things differently—and when they implement them, situations change as they become unstuck.

Or, as a client recently put it: "All I was waiting for was for permission to change, and you gave it to me. And now I realise **I** gave it to me, in your presence."

Here's an illustration of this process, and why less is never better.

A client will say, "I want to learn not to yell at my husband." I'm broke, fix me. Now, even from a superficial view of this request, you'll see the problem. Let's just say I wave my magic wand and she stops yelling. Now what will she do? She will, in a sense, be mute. You see, she doesn't have behaviour to be *stopped*. She *lacks* a behaviour that *works*.

I just took a "break" from writing this to sit with clients. They have set a 2-month time limit to sharpen, or end, their relationship. We (they, actually) have come to see that they need to commit to being with each other *as they are*, or they need to end the relationship. To be together and to do nothing other than judge each other to be inadequate is no longer an option for them.

I've impressed myself with their questions and insights. He said, "I used to upset myself that she was gone most evenings. I'd miss her, and then pick a fight when she came home. Now I miss her and enjoy our time together when she comes home."

She said, "And I'd hate coming home because he'd be angry, or so I'd tell myself. I'd come in angry and I'd turn it into a fight from there. I really like it that we've come up with a new way to do this."

I said, "And the next step is for both of you to accept the other person no matter how they are. If someone is angry, sit with them and allow them to be angry in your presence. Don't judge it, try to fix it, or anger yourself. Just be with each other, as you are."

The point is: you are, and others are "as they are." There's nothing intrinsically bad or good about any of it. It's just how it is. A minute from now, it will be some other way. If I believe that certain behaviours are "broken" and therefore unacceptable, I end up focusing only on the "broken" part, and I bitch, moan and complain about it. The other, more elegant option is to see **right now** as "how it is." If I "sit with **how it is**," it simply is, until it isn't.

I choose to surround myself with people who "get" this. This is especially true in my principal relationship with Darbella. I'm not interested in a relationship where I must "behave myself in a certain way," if that way is suggested or "demanded" by another. Since I know that Dar **chooses** to be with me, I find I am even freer to get over myself when I shift into non-productive behaviours. If I simply have my feelings and get past them (as opposed to stuffing them,) I find that I do less simmering and drama creating, and more expressing and moving past.

Letting go of seeing yourself as broken, and/or seeing others as broken flies in the face of our culture and almost seems counter-intuitive. Yet seeing ourselves as whole, complete, "good" decent people—in our entirety—is the only path I've found that actually leads to freedom and self-knowledge. I am all of me. None of me goes away. I am the totality of my experiences and am the moment-by-moment story I choose to tell me about me. I can **add** to me by learning new skills and unearthing stuck and stuffed parts of me.

There is no greater discipline than self-acceptance, and no greater "truth" than this: I am and others are exactly and precisely who they *enact*. They are not who they say they are. They are how they do life. Not broken, not whole, just human, and complete. Telling ourselves another story is just another story.

The Poignancy of the Now

I was re-watching the movie "*Waking Life*" last night. It's an odd flick, an animation over the film. The main character is caught in a dream (or dead—one character in the film says that death is an endless dream from which you can neither awake nor return to your body.)

In one scene, a woman picks up a picture of herself as a child, and says, "That's me!" To do this, the woman must tell herself a story. "I was born, and I lived here and moved there and grew up to become me."

Except her story is a convenient fiction.

There is no you other than the you that is reading this sentence right now. There is no other moment than this moment, and that has been true since the beginning of time. In fact, as Einstein proved with his Theory of Relativity, even time is a convenient yet unreal construct. We live in what philosophers call "The Eternal Now."

One "proof" of the relative elasticity of time is the dream state. You wake up at 8 am. You fall back asleep and have a rich, detailed dream of an entire day. You wake up, and it's 8:03.

In the "real" world, we've been distracted, and time flew by, or we've waited by the phone for news and time dragged. Time, in this sense, is an elastic, artificial construct.

The reason this is important is that, *without discipline*, most people spend their most of their lives immersed in the stories in their heads, and those stories point in one of two ways—past or future. Past stories are often "regret" stories, and future stories are often "catastrophe" stories. Both are used by us to create "drama and meaning" for our lives.

I do want to differentiate this kind of "pain-based" thinking from having an active fantasy life. Nothing wrong with my setting aside some time to imagine living in a tropical paradise, having sex with everyone I've ever fantasised about. I just don't want to confuse this with "reality."

The only "reality" I can ever **know** exists moment by moment. The only way I can know it is to be present in and with it. If I am sitting with you and thinking about something other than you—if I'm thinking about what I had for dinner last night or about what you really meant by something I think I remember you saying a year ago—I am no longer *present* with you. I have decided that what's going on in my head—the stories and dramas I'm telling myself—are more important (in a sense, more "real") than *you.*

I set up an experience for a couple recently. They'd been fighting about stuff, repeatedly, for years. Rather than rehash the past, I asked each of them to shift focus and state their **present** intention for the relationship. I also asked the other person to simply listen. After each stated their intention, their partner responded, "I didn't know you thought that!"

Which is sort of true. More clearly stated, it's "I was so busy up in my head, making you the bad guy, and then supporting my stance with memories I created, that I was unaware of you. I chose only to hear what would support my preconceived notion that you are a jerk."

The poignancy of the now is the somewhat rueful realisation that I am simply who I am in this moment, and who and how I "register" who I am at this moment is based entirely on how I have interpreted each of my experiences. (And this experience. And this experience. Until I die.) It also means that, if I don't like who I am in this moment, I can change my interpretations—the story I'm telling myself, right now.

In the above client illustration, the shift came as each *actively* listened—as they listened, they added to (modified) the story each was telling him or herself. This happened, as does all of life, in the moment, and has absolutely nothing to do with past experience or future expectation.

We live moment by moment, choice by choice. The past rolls up behind us (like the Langoliers roll up time in Stephen King's book, *Four Past Midnight*) and the future never is.

In other words, you have no future. Me either. All you ever have is **this moment**. This is why waiting for something to happen in the future ("and then I'll be happy!") is so stupid. Happiness, like everything else, is a moment-by-moment choice, not a future destination.

Another example: take the life of a significant person, say FDR. He's dead. So, we tell his story to remember. Except that, you can read 30 biographies, and get 30 versions of FDR. If you read his autobiography, you get another, equally strange story.

The story we tell about others is just as **subjective** as the story we tell about ourselves. There is **not** one "true" story about any person, including you. The person is the person, and that person lived one moment at a time. The person doesn't exist as a singular entity from birth to death. All that exists is moment-by-moment choice, moment-by-moment experience.

Yet another example: Admittedly, I have an internal representation of Dar. It's based on my experiences with her since 1982. Except I've only been in her physical presence a fraction of that time. (She's at work, she's away, she's asleep.) In a sense, I know *of* her, without knowing *her*. And what I know of her is totally about my *interpretation* of what I think I saw her "do." The Dar in my head is the sum of my explanations of **my** experiences with Dar.

It's just not Darbella.

So, I have certain expectations and presuppositions regarding her, but no assurances about any of it. We jokingly say we greet each other not by saying "How are you today?" but rather by saying "Who are you today?" In the end, the only "real" Dar is the one I can reach out and touch, in the here and now. The rest of the stuff in my head is me, dressing up to look like Dar.

Each moment offers us a choice—will I play in my head with my presuppositions, dramas, stories and pain, or will I be present? Am I brave enough to understand that this moment is all the time I have with Dar, and is all I will *ever* have with her? Everything else is a fiction designed to get me past scaring myself about the impermanence of my life.

One point of "*Waking Life*" is captured in the title—one can choose to wake up to life. Or, one can live forever trapped in a dreamscape, living a "life" of "woulda, coulda, shoulda." In a hundred years, no one will remember your name. No one, ever, will know you. Except, possibly, you. If you choose.

And the only you that you can know is the "you" that you are in this moment. You are not your past—all you have is a present explanation of the story you tell yourself about what you believe happened to you. In other words, you experience your past NOW and *only* now.

You are nothing more than this moment, this breath. In this moment, you can be fully alive and fully present. And in that choice, you are whole, complete and without blemish.

Authentic, enlightened living exists *only* in The Eternal Now.

Wake Up!

You exist as a part of others' imaginations

This is one of those stretchy thoughts. Imagine your father. Do a good job of it, adding "flesh to his bones" by visualizing your story about him. Now, is the father you imagined your father, or "the father you imagined?"

Just as you created an internal representation of your father, each person you know has a "you" inside of them, and they play with you inside of their heads. They watch you on their internal movie screen, they have conversations with you, and they dress and undress you. Most people assume that the "you" in their heads is an accurate representation of you. In a sense, it is. It is as accurate as they choose to make it, *for themselves.*

It just isn't you.

Nonetheless, you "exist" in the head of each person you know, just as "they" (in the form you've created for them) exist in you.

All interpersonal conflict is caused by a dilemma—my picture of you does not match my present experience of you, and I'm confused over which to trust. Here's a hint. What goes on in your head is only real for you. It's "real" because it's yours. It isn't, however, "true."

In my head are my pictures and stories. Each one is about *me*, not about their subject(s). Being conscious is knowing

the difference between the image in your head and the actual person.

When I am with Darbella, I bring with me my imaginings about Dar. I act toward her as I determine I want to act, given my notions about what kind of relationship I want to have with her. I also carry with me all the other ways I could be with her, each of which would create a different scenario.

Consciousness is knowing all of this and staying present anyway. And then, just to make it more interesting, it's knowing Dar is doing the same thing—she has brought with her all of her Waynes. Many Darbellas, many Waynes and only two of them are "real."

Here's the puzzle. What shall we choose to think of as "real?" And how do we know?

I remind myself of the games I play in my head with all the imaginary people that live in there. Then, when I move into an actual conversation or interaction with a "real" person, it would serve me well to be present with that person. It would also be "good" to remember that my presence brings along with it both my experience and all the stories I tell myself.

I am never *purely* conscious. The trick is to know this. And choose, as often as is possible, to recognise my stories and illusions.

"Reality," in this sense, is simply one more story. The actual experience was there and was gone, and each of us then categorised it and gave it meaning. Different meaning. As we are predisposed to do.

End of story.

Accepting our Emotions

One of the things the West is noted for is black and white thinking—for creating lists— "clean and dirty," "good and bad," "right and wrong." Among others. Emotions especially are divided into "good" ones and "bad" ones.

We must look to our culture to explain the phenomenon of disliking certain of our feelings, and especially disliking the "bad" ones. I emphasised the "bad" qualifier... but would hasten to note how many people also fear their good feelings. You ever hear this one? "Oh boy. I'd better stop enjoying myself this much or something bad is going to happen." The idea is that this person should only feel "neutral." Otherwise, the gods are going to even things out. After all, "This much pleasure can't be good for you." Right.

Advertising plays upon the premise that people are not happy because they *lack* something. And, "coincidentally," the lack can be fixed by buying the product being advertised. So, the average ad either directly or indirectly is saying, "Happiness is our natural state. You're not happy. Therefore, something must be wrong with you. Interestingly, and coincidentally, we have just the product that will make everything all better. Buy our car, (tampon, deodorant, dish detergent, whatever) and you will be able to do anything, be anything, be admired, smell nice and have lovely hands. And if perchance you stop feeling happy, we'll sell you more."

We believe this because we judge that we *should* be happy all the time. That everyone but us is happy all the time. Or that it's just our family that is unhappy or dysfunctional, because of the kids, or my spouse or how I was brought up. We're miserable, but no one else is. Let's buy a cure, and, as the story goes, "live happily ever after."

Nice, but it doesn't work that way, although you'd never know it by the sales racked up.

In our quest to avoid pain, we teach our kids to judge and then run away from their feelings, lest they get hurt. How silly, eh? We **know** they're going to experience hurt, yet we think we're doing them a favour by protecting them from their emotions. All we do is send them out into the world completely unprepared for failure, for pain, heartbreak, and *also* for passion. They get to figure it out by themselves.

We teach our kids and continue to reinforce in ourselves the techniques of denial and minimising. "I'm not heartbroken; I'm just a little blue today." "I'm sad, but it's not important and I'll get over it as soon as I get up and cook supper." We make our feelings small, shove them aside, and secretly judge that we are weak and stupid for having them in the first place.

The way past all of this is through honesty, openness, and the willingness to take responsibility for my choices and my emotions. Of course, I must be honest with myself before I can choose to be honest with others. It begins with the understanding that all people have feelings—emotions—feelings are happening to us all the time.

We have been trained by our culture to express certain things and suppress the rest.

A friend recently described going to a professional meeting. A new acquaintance saw her, raced over, gave her a huge hug and said, "Oh, my God. I'm so glad you're here, I just love you so much!" A hush came over the table. My friend smiled at the woman and thanked her sincerely, but the rest of the table was clearly uncomfortable. The woman, red-faced, said, "I don't know where that came from. I'm so sorry." My friend again assured her that she warmly felt the complement.

Now, what happened here is that the woman, in a moment of "loss of control," expressed clearly what she was feeling in that moment. This, however, is not something that ordinarily happens at professional gatherings in the inhibited country of Canada (nor elsewhere, truth be told.) The woman, remembering her tribal training, thoroughly embarrassed herself, simply because she let a feeling, an emotion, slip out.

My friend was not the least bothered by the emotion, as she has spent a good deal of time learning to live with and express **her own** feelings. She did what she could to be clear that she was pleased with this spontaneous expression, but the woman was already busy judging herself. And the rest of the table lapsed into uncomfortable silence, mostly, I would speculate, based upon their own projections of slipping and doing the same thing—blurting out a statement of their own passion—and then having to deal with the heat of embarrassment.

My point is this—the woman expressed what she was feeling. That intensity of feeling is our birthright and is clearly a part of us. What might life be like if we were willing to be more honest and open with such feelings? If we were to do so, we would have to stop judging our feelings and simply learn to express them.

I used the above "positive" example—the expression of an emotion most judge as positive—to demonstrate the depth of the repression of emotion that exists in our society. Let's now look at a "negative" example.

A client came in for depression management. Early on, first session, I began to speculate with him that he had an emotion expression issue, not depression. I specifically looked at his repression of anger.

Of course, he didn't succeed in *completely* blocking his anger. He blocked it until his wife came home. Then, he found something to be angry about and blasted her with the whole package. She stopped talking to him, he felt bad, apologised, and the cycle started again. He "depressed himself" over yelling at his wife, among other things.

He "regretted" his loss of control, and thought his anger "shouldn't be there."

I suggested he buy a heavy bag and pound the crap out of it. He was aghast. He was 54, he told me, and mature men don't whack heavy bags. I asked if they, instead, regularly reamed their wives a new orifice.

One day, he told me the following story: following our previous session, he had decided to perform a little test of what I was suggesting. He was not aware, he said, of feeling any anger, but decided to hit the armrest in his car. By the time he got home, he'd hit the armrest so often and so hard that he had to buy a new door panel. He said he felt his anger rise as he hit, and then dissipate, almost as if it had "left him." He also mentioned to his wife that he was considering buying a heavy bag. He expected her to be horrified. She said, "Great! When? And can I use it too?"

I don't know about you (obviously!) but when I get angry, my hand becomes a fist and I want to either hit something or yell or do both. I often yell in the car, while driving. I smack the steering wheel, and yes, I do have a heavy bag. I drive nails and dig dirt, and chop wood. All things I can put some of my aggressive energy into. I long ago decided not to stuff my anger. I also decided, pledged really, that I wouldn't direct my anger against a living thing unless physically attacked. I have dissipated most of the anger in me, so far.

Do I consider myself a "bad" person because I get angry? No, of course not. Why would I? Is that going to keep me from anger? I know that I have a wide range of emotions, and I judge that they have survived the natural selection process for a reason. Think about it. The Theory of Evolution indicates that evolution works toward strengthening what works and eliminating what doesn't, over millennia, of course. Emotions have always been a part of us. If they were superfluous, they would be gone by now. Simple as that.

If, then, we have emotions, and we are going to have emotions, what do we do with them? We, if we are wise, find ways to safely and thoroughly express them. We are complex beings with a wide range of feelings. We get sad at movies, nostalgic driving home, weepy at sunsets, inconsolable at death, ecstatic with triumph, heated with passion, orgasmic in bed—and we can literally feel all of that, and more, at the drop of a hat, in a single hour—in a single minute.

Our natural state is *not* happiness. Our natural state is awake, aware and feeling our feelings in their fullness. To be this present requires the willingness to feel everything, at maximum intensity.

Dialogue

Awareness and presence are the core of all dialogue. Dialogues are special, mostly because so few of us ever have one. Mostly we engage in sequential or simultaneous monologues.

There are only two purposes for dialogue. One is to solve a problem. The other is to share information about the only thing I can share information about—myself.

The opposite of dialogue is fighting. The difference between a dialogue and a fight is the "intent."

There are one-sided fights and two-sided fights. A one-sided fight happens when one person endlessly corrects and lectures and "persuades," while the other person says, "Yes, dear." It's a "fight" because the recipient has no intention of doing what (s)he has agreed to. You might think of it as bullying and placating.

A two-person fight is always about "who is right." Which is odd, because, as we've noted, there are only personal opinions, wants and desires. It's like that famous scene in the movie "*Annie Hall*," split screen, Woody Allen on one side, Diane Keaton on the other, each talking to their shrink. Woody: "She never wants sex—only 3 times a week." Diane: "He always wants sex—3 times a week!"

Such discussions are unsolvable, of course, because there is no "right" number of sexual encounters per week. There's just what's happening and how I interpret it. Similarly, there is no "right" way to raise a child—there's just what works. There is no "right" way to communicate—just ways that work and ways that don't.

Let's be clear here: a dialogue about an issue and a fight about who is "right" about the issue is not the same thing.

Good dialogue requires the willingness to be direct. Direct communication can be blunt communication. It is always simple communication, noticeably devoid of sub-plots or outside opinions. "Everyone knows..." is not direct. "I think..." is.

People who teach communication at The Haven often use the words "open, honest and vulnerable" to describe good communication or dialogue. They interrelate in several ways, not the least of which is this: I can only be as honest about me as my openness and vulnerability allow.

I'm amazed by how many people think that honesty is a bad thing. It's sometimes put as a power statement: "I would feel pressured if I had to tell him everything." Other times, it's a privacy issue: "I have a right to my secrets." Or an embarrassment issue: "Well, I couldn't tell *anyone* that!" Or, tit-for-tat: "I'm not going to be honest unless she is." Endless and amazing are the excuses for lying.

Darbella and I have only one "line in the sand" (a standard which, if broken, would mean the end of our relationship) and that is, total honesty. We decided, when we first started dating, and have reiterated with each other since, that honesty is not only the best policy, it's the *only* policy.

We want to remind ourselves of the point I made in the section "The Poignancy of the Now." Our commitment is to total honesty—and I can only be totally honest about what I know *today*. Thus, I agree with Gandhi, who once said something like, "I promised you the truth (as I know it today), not consistency."

I hope you begin to see how "truth" can only play out in honest, open, vulnerable dialogue. And the only "truth" I know is the truth of me, in this moment. That truth is totally encapsulated in the stories I tell myself, in the feelings I generate in myself, and in the thoughts I drive myself with. None of this "**has** to be." All of this is as I create it.

Openness is the willingness to shine a light on me. If I am open, I am willing to be clear about all aspects of myself. Vulnerability adds to this: I am even willing to admit to the scary, strange, weird, nasty, manipulative parts. I am willing to tell you how I hurt myself. I am willing to risk it because this is what true dialogue, communication and relationship require.

Of course, I get to choose who I am in true dialogue with. Many people come back from one of our Communication Workshops or from The Haven with the idea that they are supposed to be open, honest, and vulnerable, say, with the grocery clerk. This is simply not so. I might choose to be clear and honest with pretty much everyone, but that won't include sharing my inner theatre with them.

I choose open, honest vulnerability with people I trust to be so with me.

Dialogue is a tool that allows me to pay attention to myself and to share what I discover with a small and select group of friends. The real reason for the dialogue is so that someone else is witnessing what I am doing and thinking and interpreting. Then, when I get off track and lose clarity with myself, my friend(s) can call me on it, typically by asking me why I am making the choice I am making. And I can do the same for them.

Left to our own devices, we pretty much tell ourselves what we want to hear. We can get so wrapped up in the story that we miss what's "really" going on. Regular, focused dialogue is a discipline designed to commit me to being much more open about the details—the "why" in "why are you telling yourself **that** story?"

The meaningfulness of what is discussed shifts and changes; the meaning of the dialogue itself remains constant.

It is this: in dialogue, I find, listen to and reveal myself. Not for approval or validation. Only I can do that for myself. Dialogue is a way of learning ever again that I am safe being me. I am OK being me.

In the company of friends, dialogue frees us from the burden of being alone. There is, by agreement, acceptance as opposed to "right and wrong," manipulation and blame. Because, of course, there is no one to blame. There is just this moment and the next, and the story I tell. And if perchance I sadden myself with the story, I can remember Gandhi, and simply tell myself (and my friends) another one. Each equally valid. Each equally "true."

Because the only mark of the worth of a story, you see, is the result.

The Kayak

This is one of my favourite stories and is my take on an illustration David Raithby used in a workshop at The Haven.

My life consists of me, sitting in my one-person kayak. I am bobbing along, paddling along, on a relatively calm ocean, in the dark. I do not know where I am, or where I am going. I am "present" in the paddling, and nowhere else, as there *is* nowhere else.

Every now and again, I meet up with another paddler, and we get to choose whether to paddle together. We still don't know where we are or where we are going, but we are no longer lonely. I am, however, and this is key, still **alone**.

A single kayak is an interesting boat. There is only room for one. No one can climb in with me, no one can take over for me, and no one can paddle my kayak for me. I am alone in my kayak, even if other boats surround me. Whining about how unfair all of this is, how I need help, how I want someone to please take over for me, isn't going to accomplish anything, as no one can step in and bail me out.

What I *can* do is watch others paddle, and they can watch me. I can learn from others, and others can learn from me. Now, someone watching me paddle will see how I do it, and then they might try to duplicate my stroke, from their boat. The best they will ever do, however, is their version of my paddle stroke. They can't be me; they can't be like me. They can only watch and learn and do it their way.

This is the reality of life: we are born and die alone, and the rest of life is a solo job in a crowd. This is either terrifying or freeing. I'll scare myself with it precisely to the degree that I refuse to accept responsibility for my life. I will free myself precisely to the degree that I allow myself the personal satisfaction of paddling just a little more efficiently and effortlessly each day.

There will be calm days and stormy days, and days when I'm swamped and flipped over. I can drown or I can get right side up. Whining about how unfair that is only delays getting back to paddling, which is the only "truth" of my life.

In other words, I can see my life as a lesson in elegant paddling and I can learn all there is to learn about paddling well. A silly choice would be to feel sorry for myself that I must paddle. Another silly choice would be to spend my days assigning blame to others for not rescuing me or teaching me "right," or for "abusing me" by not treating me as special or whatever. For the ultimate in silly, I can simply give up, depress myself and stop paddling—and get blown wherever the wind takes me.

Deciding to paddle well, to accept that "the way it is, is the way it is," is the enlightened choice. I want to be the best me I can be, and that's totally about me—about what I choose to learn and do.

Further, I can choose to paddle with others who get this, and the paddle will be full of sharing and compassion and learning. Or I can choose to paddle alone and learn more of me.

I mean, what other option is there? It's not like griping about "how life is" changes anything, after all. You have noticed that, haven't you??

There's the joy of the paddle and smart vs. dumb choices. The dumb choice is to make a drama out of the paddle and make myself miserable.

And isn't it funny that most people pick drama over the joy of the paddle?

Self-actualized vs. Self-absorbed

Our egos want us to be *special*, to get attention; our egos are on us relentlessly—judging us as failures while spurring us on to repeat the stuff our egos judge us for.

This causes us to become self-absorbed—to get locked into relentless self-flagellation.

On the other hand, the self-actualized person is able, repeatedly, to step out of this game.

Here are a few differences between being self-actualized and being self-absorbed.

- The self-actualized person understands that his own world revolves around himself.
- The self-absorbed person thinks the whole world revolves around her.
- The self-actualized person asks, "What can I learn?"
- The self-absorbed person asks, "What's in it for me?"

We've been conditioned to elevate ourselves to unreal levels. We annoy ourselves over others we judge "too big for their britches," missing our own games and judgements. One way past this is to see self-absorption for what it is—a diversion designed to keep us stuck in irrelevant stories.

We let go of our games through self-knowing and self-actualization.

The self-absorbed person expects to be put first

The self-absorbed person believes that he lives at the centre of the universe, thinks that everything should go exactly as he wants it to and that anything and everything that is happening is about him. He is highly opinionated, thinks he's the smartest person in the room and thinks that he is always "right," always justified in his behaviour. When he judges that someone is not considering him first, he redoubles his effort to be noticed. In a traffic jam, the self-absorbed person asks, "Why is this happening to me?"

The problem with self-absorption

If I am trying to be the centre of *everyone else's* attention, I have no centre to call my own. If I am using my sexuality or talents to try to "win love," I am using rather than valuing myself. If I have the expectation that love means that another person is going to meet my every need, take care of me, and put me ahead of everything else, eventually, I'm going to be very disappointed.

I'm using self-absorbed to describe a way of being

Self-absorption is both a mental perspective and an action. Another, clinical definition of being self-absorbed is being a *narcissist*. The narcissist craves *external* validation—in other words, I am nothing if I am not noticed.

Everything the person does is done to gain attention. My mom had this perspective. I can't number the times when what she wanted was at cross purposes with what she was getting, and she would literally puff herself up to her full, towering 5'

0", and thunder, "How can they do this? Don't they know who I am?"

The self-actualized person takes her own wants *seriously*.

She knows herself and seeks to know more. She never assumes that she's "done" with much of anything—never is there a sense of "been there, done that," because she knows that the "there" and the "that" are constantly changing. If something isn't going the way she wants it to, she simply stops doing what isn't working, without whining or complaining, and does something else.

The self-actualized person has learned to be self-sufficient.

They are not in need (not needy) of the support of others. This comes from a place of self-responsibility. They do not require *an audience* to feel valuable—they already value themselves as they are. They may *choose* to be entertaining—and many have great charisma. They work from a place of great enjoyment of the drama and the beauty of life.

Self-actualization is about self-knowledge, coupled with letting others off the hook

The self-actualized person does what he does because he derives satisfaction from a job well done. He works from a calm centre and finds value from his active engagement with the world—with the situation at hand. The person's self-esteem is not dependent on the views, actions, or reactions of others.

A Recap and a Metaphor

The self-actualized person has the keys to her own car, turns her key all by herself, and drives where she chooses. She does as she chooses, in keeping with her values and principles. She is content to be the centre of attention of a crowd of one. She is aware of herself, content with herself, and willing to bring herself forward in full engagement with others and the world.

The self-absorbed person wants you to admire his car, to care about (or even want to go along!) where he is driving to, and to be responsible for keeping track of his keys. He wants others to take time out of their day to deliver his lost keys, wants to be told how much he'll be missed, and then to be sent on his way with his GPS fully programmed for him.

The self-absorbed person wants everyone to stand on the side of the road and wave as he goes by. He imagines the crowds whispering to each other, "I wonder where he is off to now?" And of course, he wants congratulations for figuring things out (they often imagine that they are very bright...)—simple things, like finding his way back home.

The self-absorbed person is sure life is about getting attention, so the self-absorbed person seeks a good publicist.

For the self-actualized person, it's all about completing legs on a journey that never ends. Self-actualization takes nerve, bravery, and self-assurance.

The self-actualized person knows herself well, likes herself, seldom second-guesses herself, and cheerfully lives with the consequences of her actions. She seeks the ways and means of meeting her own needs and engaging joyfully in the lives of others, without attempting to manipulate others into being more focussed on her than on their own walks.

Life becomes an adventure, fully expressed and felt. A bit more about this in the next section.

On Being Self Centred

Many clients have trouble with me and my way of understanding. I often begin counselling by saying, "The hardest part of what I'm going to suggest to you is this: I teach self-responsibility and letting go of blame. There's nothing happening to you, no one is doing anything to you, and where your life is right now is totally and completely the result of your choices and interpretations."

Somehow, many people manage to twist that around into "You want me to only think of myself!!!" I could argue that that is precisely all we *can* think about, but I know what they mean. They mean that thinking about themselves is selfish. And they learned from mommy and daddy that being selfish is a bad, bad thing.

So, I want to help you get past this.

As we are socialised, our first black and white thought—that I "should" be first, is replaced with the equally black and white thought that everyone else is more important than me.

We learned both approaches as part of the ego project and neither is particularly helpful.

I attempt to teach each client to continually bring their centre of attention back into their *self* (the true meaning of self-centered.)

You do *not* do this to demand that others place their centre in you and put you first. You do this to remind yourself that the only place you "are"—and the only place the world is—for you, is inside of you. Each of us is totally responsible for ourselves and how we choose to live our lives. Period. And that's all self-centered means.

What typically happens for those who adopt this view is that they stop taking responsibility for other people's dramas—and that pisses those folk right off. Many, many people are looking for others to fix their problems; others seek people to blame for their misery.

When you opt out of the rescuing role, they are left with the sickening feeling that maybe their distress is about their own approach to life, and they get scared or angry. They then try to persuade you to go back to your old way of behaving—to take care of them or take responsibility for their pain.

One of the best "persuaders" is to pull the "you're being selfish" card.

Learning not to bite—on guilt, obligation, blame or "you're being selfish"—is a skill mastered by practice. And thank god, when you start being self-centered and self-responsible, those around you will step up and give you all the practice you need.

What I see in my life (and in the lives of the clients I've worked with who adopt this perspective and way of being) is that, far from being *selfish*, they are open, honest, full of life and endlessly willing to "demonstrate good paddling."

A client asked me if I don't get tired of repeating this message to clients, and said, "I'd get really pissed off if I had to say it to someone twice." He got the joke that I've said it to **him** more than twice.

I replied that I am only interested in whether the person expresses some interest in self-responsibility. If they are willing to work toward understanding self-responsibility *and* adopting it as a life-choice, I'll stick around with them forever. If they are not interested, I'll pull back, decrease contact or end contact. Simple as that.

I do what I do because I'm endlessly curious about people and their choices. I consider myself blessed that I have people in my life who have taught this to me. I remember my therapist Gloria Taylor saying, "Teach this to 10 people—that's your obligation to me for teaching it to you." I get what she's saying.

I listen to myself as I counsel (and write this book) and I learn from me. Or better, I re-mind me. I reprogram myself for self-responsibility. I want others to find a way to their self-responsibility—I love watching as their curiosity, compassion and understanding grow. Not selfish, not other focused—simply in the moment, sharing their experience, watching, and being curious.

It's like in the *Kayak* story. I know how to paddle "better" (more elegantly) than my client. Why else would they be there? I'm not about to waste a lot of time asking them how to "fix what ails them." *If they knew how they'd have fixed it.* I'm there to teach them new ways of seeing, understanding and most of all, enacting what they learn in the real world. The relationship is 'teacher to student.'

In my close friendships and especially with Darbella, it's a meeting of equals and a sharing of stories, interpretations, and curiosity.

Selfish? Self-aggrandizing? If you choose to see it that way. I don't. I see my life moment by moment, and I don't have forever, so I don't have a ton of time for drama. I know what I know, and I choose how I live, consistently, on that basis. I don't "do" dysfunctional relationships, nor act like an idiot, any more than I "have to."

In the end, if you "get this," you'll find yourself living out your life in a conscious, present, honest, and curious way. You'll take what comes without judgement and decide what you choose to do next. You will be consistent and clear. And you will be that most unique (yet not special) of all humans—a self-responsible person, engaged in living life to the fullest while extending an invitation to others to join you in the paddle, the dance.

Drama

"Drama" is my present favourite word for all the "problems" people bring to my office. My usage is not "negative." Rather, it is a comment on one's life focus. Thus, perhaps the opposite of "drama" is "reality."

People whose lives are one drama after another are often described as *Drama Queens.*

- We have one friend who, when in drama queen mode, runs from room to room, arms akimbo, flapping and flailing, voice strident, and everything is described in absolutes.

- My mom used to do drama queen by quivering her lip and endlessly explaining how she was "so sick, the sickest person on the planet." And no one, **no one**! was treating her right.
- One of my male clients does drama by crossing his arms across his chest, sliding lower on the couch, lowering the tone of his voice, and squinting his eyes as he lectures menacingly.
- My own personal favourite "drama queen" tack is to go to "poor abused little boy, hard done by." I get, at the same time, whiny and indignant. I got this way through practice—through my choices regarding my upbringing. I am an only child, and a long-awaited one to boot. (My parents were 39 and 35 when I was born.) I was doted upon and was given anything I asked for. Imagine my surprise when I grew up, went off to University and was treated as normal as opposed to special. I reacted by learning to rant, rave and blame (sounds like a law firm...) In short, I act like a 6-year-old mid-tantrum.

If you were watching my face right now, you'd see that my right eyebrow is pulled up (my "irony" look) and you'd see a small rueful smile on my face. And I just sighed.

My sigh says it all. I would dearly love to assure you that I'll never pull the "little kid, hard done by" act, ever again. I *can't* assure you of that because I am me, and I will do drama queen again. What I can do is get good at noticing the drama I'm creating for myself, own it, get through the drama queen act quickly and efficiently, and even give Dar a minute or two of warning that I intend to go there.

I'm rueful because I know I'm not alone in wanting such silliness to simply go away. In fact, that's what many people think therapy is for.

Here's the way it is: I can't eliminate what I don't like about myself, but I can control how I *express* it.

In a sense, drama queen behaviour has a lot in common with acting. You hear actors talking about "stepping into role," and "Method Actors" will, for example, gain or lose weight and otherwise modify their bodies to match the character. An actor steps into the character, yet without losing sight of the stark reality: no matter how well they play the role, they are not the role. Acting is called acting because it's all an act.

We think it's harder to make the distinction in our personal lives, at the level of our internal theatre. It's not. All that's required is presence.

To *consciously* enter into and examine our drama requires force of will and a devotion to being present. The presence part helps us to determine several things, not the least of which is, "What am I trying to accomplish here?"

During the year I put in as a hospital chaplain, I saw lots of strange behaviour. Parents would get emotionally drawn into the drama (it was a Children's Hospital) and that's completely natural. What was weird was that they'd often take their dramas out on the doctors and nurses. Now, yes, the medical staff is trained not to "bite" on such displays, but they too are human, and the more arrogant, angry and blaming the parents were, the more the care and compassion exhibited toward their kid diminished. I would take the parents aside, to a quiet room (what a joke!) and encourage them to vent at me, at the couch, at the wall. Then they could go and *talk* with the staff.

Drama in and of itself isn't bad. Drama aimed at someone else almost always gets us precisely the opposite of what we want.

I know. You're thinking, "But...but... why can't people cut me some slack? I'm emotionally wrought up, and they should just overlook it!" Now, get your little lip to tremble, and look pitiful. Great.

They won't do it because "Drama Queen mode" is annoying, not endearing. Or they will do it, and try to "make you" feel guilty. Or they'll do what you ask and create their own "martyr" drama. (There's nothing worse than trying to live with a martyr.)

Ram Dass once said that he had spent his life doing "nobody special training." Drama's cure is precisely this.

I may have internal dramas and I may even choose to enact one or two, but they are nothing special, nor am I. If I can include my drama in my self-definition, without judgment, my dramas will, quite quickly, become less dramatic. And by suspending judgment, I can simply be who I am, at this moment. I can be sad when sad, happy when happy, horny when horny, bored when bored.

It's like "Hmm. I notice I am boring myself. Do I want to fix it or just be bored?" Not much drama there. As opposed to, "Oh! Shit! I'm soooooo bored. I must be the most bored person on the planet. I'm surrounded by boring losers so no wonder I'm bored! Why don't they get off their asses and be exciting??? Woe is me!!"

Same boredom, different drama. You pick, you choose.

Getting the Joke

There's a certain amusing irony to life. When I am caught in my drama, I am deadly serious. Yet, the less I cling, the more I laugh. The joke is understood and appreciated by fully embracing the ultimate absurdity of our lives. "Life is a purposeless drift," so live it fully. Get it? Now, isn't that a slice?

Or, "Wherever you go, there you are." There's no escape, no "Everything will be better when..." There's no, "I'll be happy when I find a new dance partner."

And then there's paradox. Life is suffering, the Buddha tells us. And it's also bliss. Only I can live my life, and I can also find myself in a relationship. I can only do what I do, and yet service and compassionate action are the ultimate sources of connection. In the midst of life, we are in the midst of death, so live! The ego must die for you to be who you are. And on and on.

Irony heaped upon irony.

A lot of this has been reduced to slogans— "Have an attitude of gratitude," "Be Here Now," "Today is the first day of the rest of your life." Whatever. And because of this, we tend to throw out the message with the slogan. Yet this timeless idea, this timeless joke re-presents itself to us in each ironic turn of phrase, each event that we chose to *really* see, and each interaction at its depth.

I watched "*American Beauty*" a few weeks ago, likely for the 10th time. The entire movie is about getting the joke. It starts by profiling an entirely dysfunctional family living out their days in mindless tedium, placing value on possessions, arguing and disengaging and blaming. Then, dad sees his "American Beauty," and decides to shift his being. He quits his job, gets healthy, gets high, gets horny. By the end of the movie, the protagonist knows that he's whole. His last "on the earth" words are "Boy, oh boy, oh boy!"—delivered with a smile.

In his soliloquy at the end, he says,

> "I guess I could be pretty pissed off about what happened to me... but it's hard to stay mad when there's so much beauty in the world. Sometimes I feel like I'm seeing it all at once, and it's too much. My heart fills up like a balloon that's about to burst... And then I remember... to relax, and not try to hold on to it. And then it flows through me like rain. And I can't feel anything but gratitude for every single moment of my stupid little life. You have no idea what I'm talking about, I'm sure. Don't worry... you will someday."

He got the joke. He started *living* his life instead of *watching* it. He did what he did for the moment and engaged passionately in each second.

Someday, we all get to "get" it. And here's the joke: the day you get it is the day you *choose* to get it, **or** at the moment of your death. If you get it now and live it now, you will feel... everything. Which, I believe, is why you incarnated. So, what are you waiting for?

Embrace it all, and smile.

Waiting for Godot

Beckett's famous, absurdist play is about only one thing—waiting. The two guys spend the entire play—waiting for Godot. The talk about what they'll do when Godot arrives. They discuss the amazing experiences they'll have. Fun, fun, fun, once Godot gets there. By the end of the first act, it's apparent Godot isn't going to show up. So, what do they do?

They come back the next day and wait some more. At the end of the play, there they sit, still waiting.

Which begs the question: what are **you** waiting for?

In the endless stream of eternity, *This Endless Moment* is all that there is. The elements of yin/yang— the dance of light with dark, hot with cold, good with bad—this *interplay* exists only in this moment. This being said, what are **you** waiting for?

Does it appear that I think this question is important? Good. It is.

I watch people piss their lives away, toiling, struggling, whining—and waiting. They've told themselves a story about how once "Godot" arrives, all will be well. Yet this is a double-edged sword. If like in the play, Godot never arrives, then that's why they're not happy. Or, if Godot arrives and nothing changes, it's Godot's fault.

Choosing to live life in this moment and the next, on the other hand, is what self-responsibility is all about, in practical terms. Nothing to wait for, no fault, no blame. Just living each moment, fully and completely.

What are you waiting for?

Driving Forces

Most people seem to have lost a sense of purpose. Most 'mid-life crisis' is a reaction to this lost sense.

Young people assume that career and marriage will do the trick for them. Then, by their late thirties, they may conclude that one or the other is all that is possible. The crunch of the 40 to 50 crowd is the sudden realisation that pretty much *nothing* they've put emphasis on is panning out as they expected. This desolate realisation leads many to my counselling office.

I suspect that societal propaganda leads to much of this. There's a belief that career and family will magically provide meaning. It's ironic and sad when people hit the wall at 50—they discover that despite having focused on living the life society promotes, satisfaction eludes them.

A 48-year-old woman started therapy yesterday and said that she'd been unhappy for the entire 28 years of her marriage. Nothing worked for her—not the communication, the sex, the concept of common goals. She had a job to go to, and nothing else. Yet, her description was almost completely about how sad and depressed her *husband* was. When I asked how *she* was, she looked at me blankly and changed the subject.

She's not so unusual. Another client described her life prior to therapy as "living by the book." She said, "You know. The book. The one that tells you, 'do this, think that,' and gives you all the answers. I believed there was such a book, and that I just must be stupid because my life was so miserable. I was trying so hard to follow the rules and nothing was working.

Now I realise that I was slavishly acting out a role and hadn't a clue about me."

She is still exploring who she is and how she is and what she wants—a decidedly new project. In a sense, she is creating, for the first time, an independent identity based on self-reflection, as opposed to basing her identity upon what she imagines she "ought" to be doing, or upon what the "significant males" in her life tell her to do or be.

As usual, there is a paradox here. If I choose, my focus can be exactly and precisely upon what *society* values—for example, I can decide that being a high-powered, rich executive is what I want. The paradox revolves around the difference between ***choosing*** vs. simply and mindlessly pursuing such a direction because 'everyone is doing it.'

Using marriage as an example, most people who get married simply get married, with no thought about what kind of marriage they want. If asked, they'll say, "A happy one," or "One that lasts forever." When you ask for specifics, out comes the lame, blank look. They assume that "everyone knows what a successful marriage looks like," and "it just happens."

Well, no, it doesn't.

Blind luck is a stupid thing to trust your life to. Having the life that you want requires focus, dedication and, first, an actual understanding of what, specifically, you want.

As I continue to insist in this book, there is nothing more important than being awake, present and self-responsible. In no area is this more important than in the arena of how you live out your life—what some have called "the path of purpose."

To just blindly stumble along, trying this, sampling that, learning nothing, and having minimal or no satisfaction is not exactly a trip I'd choose to take. Yet, most people, when asked, are good at listing what they *don't* want, abysmal failures at identifying and declaring what they *do* want.

Last night, I asked a client to say what she thought about a suggestion her husband had just made. She said, "I don't necessarily disagree with it." I complimented her on totally avoiding responsibility for answering. She laughed and called me a "smart ass."

The main reason for not being specific—for not "owning" the choices we are making, for playing the "I'm just doing what I'm supposed to be doing," card—is to escape responsibility, while living on autopilot and believing in luck.

Owning and clarifying my sense of purpose, my commitment to principles, my approach to communication—all of this is self-responsible behaviour.

I'm not going to get into a rant about which driving forces or guiding principles "should" be on your list. Frankly, I don't know and don't particularly care. My goal is to get you to look at how much of your life has been given over to autopilot—to putting in time without any sense of direction, plan, or purpose. Or, to get you to notice that you **do** declare principles yet aren't **living** what you declare to be your principles.

I hate excuses, and I'm not much of a fan of unreflective, uncommitted living either. Think about what drives you, what your purpose is, what you want and where you are headed.

If it seems like life is aimlessly flowing by, get a grip on yourself, and take the time to commit to something. Then, live it!

You Can't Have It All — The Perils of Entitlement

This is another one of those, "Yeah, I know that" points that most of us resist. In other words, we agree in principle that "we" can't, but "I" assume that "I" can.

Unbelievably, the idea of entitlement is a recent phenomenon. Honestly striving for success, on the other hand, is a cornerstone of the West. To use an American analogy, there's always been a belief in the Horace Greeley/Horatio Alger *American Dream* myth— "if I "go West," I'll conquer the world, turning rags-to-riches." We'll leave aside the part about killing any non-white person in the way. Pretty much all of us in North America "got here" because our forebears believed this idea.

I believe it too. Hard work, more often than not, pays off. Education, more often than not, pays off. Focus and commitment... well, you get it.

Where all of this went off the rails was after WWII. From out despair that was the "dirty 30s" to the trenches to the return to "normalcy," came the stunning idea that the American Dream was there for the *receiving.* (Notice I didn't say "earning.") Entitlement replaced honest toil and striving.

We saw the myth played out on TV shows like "Father Knows Best." I'm old enough to remember watching that show—the mischievous kids who got into trouble, took their issues to dad, watched him light his pipe and spout wisdom and smoke in equal measure. Mom would flit in, crinoline crinkling, with a cup of coffee, and a "Now, dear..." and offer her two cents. Successful in business, happily married, and the perfect parent of exactly one boy / one girl, both "just great!"

Yowzer!

A seed was being planted in the collective psyche. Because of the wealth and the jobs that were available after WWII, it seemed that indeed everything was possible. We saw this fictionalised family and thought it was real—*a couple of generations of us thought it was our right to be successful in all areas.*

So, we tried to have it all. There was an immediate time crunch, so we threw "stuff" at our spouses and kids, to make up for the lack of communication and "face time." What we created was the monster we may never be able to kill—entitlement.

The kids growing up in this mess did not know hardship, although all of their parents had. The parents were depression babies or teens, and they had seen the other side. This was not going to happen to their kids!

Most parents, to this day, fear any form of hardship for their kids. I was watching Doctor Phil the other day. He was talking to a 27-year-old who was jobless, girlfriend-less and living with his mommy. He spent his days playing the guitar. Doctor Phil asked the mom why she didn't kick him out so he'd learn to be independent. She replied, "I don't want him living under a bridge."

Doctor Phil replied, "Better now than when he is 40!"

The guy smirked throughout. He knows mom isn't going to kick his sorry ass out. Besides, he imagines that he has rights—her house is his house, and he's entitled to sit on said ass and be looked after. Doctor Phil suggested he spend a full working day looking for work. Quoth the "kid," "You sound just like my mom!" Smirk.

I wanted to slap him across the face. I got so disgusted I turned off the set.

Entitlement is the expectation that I deserve to be given special treatment—that I *deserve* to be given whatever I think I need. And even more deadly—that all of this is my birthright.

I can't tell you how many clients have come in, totally frustrated, because "It's not working out right!" They expected to be happy—happily married, with great kids and a terrific career, cars, houses, stuff, and lots of free time to enjoy it. And, by god, it's not happening! The kids have problems, the spouse is sleeping on the couch, work is a drag, the boss is a jerk and the roof leaks on the mortgaged-to-the-hilt house.

Big sigh, pained look, and a shake of the head. Then, the head lifts, eyes lock on mine and verbally or non-verbally I hear, "Fix it!"

Right.

You may have gathered that I think that the "fix," such as it is, is persistent self-responsible behaviour. There is no magic cure, no course you can take, no book you can read (including this one!) that will "make it all better." There is no "it" to make better. There is my life, and there are my choices. And one of the hardest ones is this: "What will I choose to focus on, this time around?"

It's hard enough to learn to do any one of these things well, let alone have the expectation that all areas "should" work out, somehow with minimal effort. And yet, that's what I hear. "I don't want a hassle when I get home. I work hard. (S)he should understand and cut me slack." And (s)he is thinking the same thing. And the kids, god bless 'em, having had stuff tossed at them out of guilt by under-involved parents, expect the world—and parents' schedules—to revolve around them. Now, can you guess why, when the precious little dears get to be adults, they don't want to move out, or if they do, expect to be looked after and coddled by their partner—their teachers—their boss?

The way out of this mess is to take a big step back. We have friends we consider excellent parents. Their 14-year-old skates. When she wants to do something else, they say, "Great! We'll cancel the skating lessons, and you can do that!" She sighs and drops the new request, as she loves skating. They insist that she focus in and do well. Entitlement crashes on the floor in their house, regularly.

What a concept! Pick something and do it until you are proficient at it! Reward your kids with your presence and involvement, as opposed to "stuff." Spend daily, quality time with your significant other, in actual dialogue. Expect to look after yourself, not to be doted upon.

In short, get over yourself, get off your ass and get a life. Happiness—it's not your right, and no one owes it to you, and... here it comes... it's *earned*!

Or I guess you could go live with your mommy.

The Fixer-Upper

Almost all the dysfunctional conversations I've listened to follow this pattern: one person starts by listing off the sins... real and imagined... *of their partner.* And then! Miracle of miracles! The speaker starts listing off exactly what the *other person* needs to do to "get fixed up!"

It's a bloody miracle, how perceptive these people are... about what the *other person's* failings are, about what the *other person* does to break communication, about how the *other person* doesn't call enough, or calls on the wrong schedule, or wants *them* to do things differently.

I especially amuse myself over the latter one.

Before I retired, I'd be working with a couple, and one of them would start presenting his or her list of the sins, omissions, and commissions... of their partner.

Typically, the other person would jump in with a "...if you think that's bad, just wait until you hear what (s)he does!"

Sometimes I'd cut it off quickly, sometimes I'd let it play out. I wasn't however, *interested* in any of it.

One of my favourite things, though, was to let them go for a bit, then turn to whoever started, and say, "So, if I'm following you, what you want is for him/her to change his ways. To shift his behaviour... to do things your way. Right?"

Thinking I was on board, I'd get a big smile and a nod.

"So," I'd continue, "why don't *you* just stop what you're doing and change your behaviours to go along with what **(s)he** wants? (S)he was pretty clear..."

And boom, I was the new target.

"But... but, that's nuts! (S)he's wrong and (s)he needs to change! That's why I brought him/her here... so you could fix him/her! I told you my house was a fixer-upper!!"

Well, not the last line, but the rest of it.

Not once in 32 years did I hear, "Jeez, you're right! I'm trying to change him; he's trying to change me. Why do I think my way is right... for him?" (And vice versa, of course.)

All of this happens because people are dumb, and think others are fixer-uppers.

I was guilty of this during my second marriage, (thanks be that I smartened up for round three, as Darbella is not noted for suffering fools...)

Oh, phooey, let me tell you a bit of that story.

I met "Sue" (I've told this story in booklets and maybe in one of my books, and I call her "Sue," so I'll use that pseudonym here) in college. The college did semesters in a 4-1-4 plan, and January was either a one course intensive, or a month off. In January of 1972 I was at good old Elmhurst College, but not taking a course. I was very, very bored.

One afternoon I wandered into the College Bookstore, and there she was: 5'2", blond-haired, blue-eyed, tight sweater and toothy smile. I was smitten, otherwise known as "lust-struck." Long story short, I asked her out.

One thing led to another, and we ended up dating, then living together. It was a rocky relationship—lots of difficulties—we broke up 3 times in 2 years. Then, she'd show up wearing cut-offs and a tube top, and I'd be all lust-struck again.

Despite all of this, we got engaged in 1975. I remember her asking me whether I was going to propose, and I remember thinking, "Don't do it. Run!" Then the other side of my head said, "But you have **3 years** invested. You can always change her!" So, I proposed.

See? Dumb.

I couldn't change *her*, of course, but I spent 7 years of trying to. Finally, with a fresh counselling degree in my back pocket, I ended things.

I wasn't impressed with myself. I knew back in 1975 that my choice to propose was based on fluff and tube tops. I went for it anyway, thinking that my way of seeing things would "win out."

Fortunately, I learned my lesson.

During counselling training, I'd learned a good communication model and much better ways of relating... none of it had *anything* to do with changing the *other person*. What it did have to do with was respect, and with being with another person—**exactly as they are**.

And I learned a way to talk that leads to issue resolution. Not *fixing* the other person. *Issue* resolution.

That was hard for me, as my default position is to assume that I am both smart and "right." So, to shift to this new approach, I first had to rein in my ego.

To recap, I initially dated "Sue" because I found her attractive (a pretty normal reason to go out on a date.) Even after getting to know her and realising we were *not compatible*, I decided to stick around and "fix her up," rather than move on.

You wouldn't believe how many people I know who are in relationships precisely for this reason and are either in the process of divorcing or have moved to separate bedrooms.

Dumb. Just dumb.

I'm glad I finally learned from my mistakes.

I wrote my book *Find Your Perfect Partner* to describe a key to resolving this. It involves... wait for it... waking up and paying attention. You can learn to decide *exactly* what kind of person you want to be in a relationship with, and then to find that person.

I then wrote *The. Best. Relationship. Ever.* This book is all about how to communicate, how to be a true partner, and how to have the relationship you want.

And... it only took me three marriages to figure this stuff out.

You must decide what the basis of your relationship is.

- It can't be, "She's not right for me, but I can fix her."
- It can't be, "He gives me great orgasms." (Unbelievably, one client told me that was the *sole* reason she'd married her ex-husband. 6 months later, she got a divorce.)
- It can't be, "I don't want to be alone, so (s)he's better than nothing."

People aren't fixer-uppers.

If you and your partner, after serious effort, are still not landing on the same page about the purpose of relating, leave. Just get up and go. Then, do a better job articulating what you want your next relationship to look like, and hold out until you find someone with similar ideas.

Because fixer-uppers often turn into time and money pits. And life is short.

Ways Inside:
Eastern Approaches

While I hope you'll choose to read my "Eastern" book, *Half Asleep in the Buddha Hall,* I couldn't resist dropping in a few eastern concepts. As you'll read, they mesh quite well with being self-responsible and awake.

The Illusion of a Self

In Buddhism, there is the concept of no-self, which is related to the idea of emptiness. No-self does *not* mean that no one exists; it means that we exist apart from our definitions. This is scary, as we've been conditioned from birth to have a fixed identity.

We attach permanence to everything, which is why we get all *bent* when things (stuff, others, ourselves) change. Attaching permanence regarding "who we are" begins right after we are born, and people start telling us about ourselves:

"You are Wayne, you are male, you are a Protestant, you are smart, cute, you are able to do stuff really well, etc."

"You are Sally, you are female, Catholic, not so smart, a tad homely, you can't do much, but if you agree to do what men want you to do, you'll get by."

Whatever

The people who told us this stuff held the power of life and death over us—so we assumed (not knowing any better) that they must *know something.* We accepted and absorbed their descriptions of us (and how the world works) as if it were not only "*true*" but the only possible truth.

As we got older, we took over the job; we build upon their creation by *adding in our own stuff*—how we see ourselves, what works for us, what doesn't—and the result is what 'I' call 'me.'

Except it's not "real"—or "true." It is, however, a *story*.

It takes great effort, but if you pay attention, you will see that your story is simply a construction. A fiction. Or better, one "truth" among many.

A client told me this story: when she was growing up, she'd *never* received a compliment or praise. She said that she still wasn't. This was a **fixed belief**—a part of her "me" story.

During therapy, she learned to pay attention, to listen without presuppositions, and to challenge her beliefs. One day, she *heard* a compliment. She watched herself as she attempted to *disregard* the complement—to deny it, to pretend it hadn't happened. She fought this urge, and let the warmth of the compliment wash over her.

By the *next week*, she was hearing lots of compliments and was also remembering ones she'd received in the past. She realised that her "I never receive compliments" belief was simply a filter. This belief filtered out—discounted—her *hearing* compliments.

We see ourselves and what is happening around us through our *filters*—through the stories and beliefs we have about ourselves.

When we make a profound shift in our *self*-understanding, all that happens is that we drop the old, dysfunctional belief, and we apply the *new* filter.

But then we forget the filter lesson we just learned and boldly declare, "This is *really* me!"

Nope. The odd, scary, interesting truth is that you are always and only *how* (not who) you are *right now*. There is no fixed entity I can point to, no "Wayne." I'm a process, not a fixed entity.

Analogy alert!

It's like this: I am a scrapbook, and so are you. My mom and dad started the scrapbook, filling it with 'images' (beliefs) of what they liked about me. Or better, they filled it with stories about what they *valued*. I was "lucky" because they mostly filled it with "good" stuff, but still, the early pages contain *only the things (the aspects of me) they approved of* or thought were valuable.

Even though it was my scrapbook, I, not knowing any better, bought into this scrapbook; I declared it "true," I adopted it as 'Wayne,' and I carried it around with me, without having done anything resembling analysis about what they valued.

Then, *I* started adding stuff.

When I was a kid, I followed *their* patterns—I added, or included the things they had taught me to value. As I got older, I "rebelled" and began to add stuff they didn't approve of.

Then I added "adult" stuff, relationship stuff, sex stuff, career stuff, etc. And not just biographical data. More importantly, I added my beliefs about my worth, and condensed it all down into "This is who I am."

At 65, I have a big, big scrapbook, with 'Wayne' written on the cover. See? Me!!!

And all around me, in piles so high that they cannot be fathomed, is all the stuff that has happened that I've *ignored* or *rejected*. That stuff makes up multiple alternate versions of the "reality" of me—I'm all of that too, even though I haven't chosen to add it to the 'Wayne' scrapbook.

And then, hidden in a locked room is another pile of stuff that I am *unaware of*. This is stuff that didn't fit with the story I was telling myself at the time, or I was afraid to deal with it, so I buried it before it registered.

Here's a positive example of this kind of blindness:

I remember finding, then Facebook friending a guy I knew back in College. I thanked him for teaching me to appreciate

Jazz and the Blues, something that shifted my musical preferences permanently.

That was what I remembered of our relationship.

Imagine my surprise when he replied and spoke with some emotion about all *I'd* done for *him*—specifically, for teaching him to process B&W film and to appreciate art.

I'd *completely forgotten* both of those things, things that were of *profound* importance to him. They were *absent*—they were not a part of my scrapbook—although they are now.

The reason 'getting' this is so important is that **we are not a fixed entity**, but are more like water. We are flowing along, clear (even fixated) on some stuff, oblivious to other stuff.

You and I are made up of *everything* we have seen, heard, and done, and we are all the things we've conditioned ourselves to ignore or suppress. Just like the woman who didn't hear compliments, and who later discovered she was swimming in them.

If we invest the time and energy to explore ourselves, and to hold our scrapbooks loosely, we might just discover that far from being limited and unhappy, we are much more broadly capable than we imagine.

Our goal is to acknowledge that we've been conditioned to miss the depth and breadth of ourselves and then to work on repairing this by *paying attention*.

If we say stuff like "That's how I am" and then limit ourselves from acting differently, well, that's kind of silly. If we become fluid and elegant, we might just choose to grab on with both hands to a larger version of our *story*.

See if you can hold your self-story loosely, and experiment with being a *process*, as opposed to a scrapbook.

What is Being Awake?

The Buddha, when asked who he was (what set him apart) said, "I am awake." I imagine it could strike you as being a bit odd, all this talk of *becoming* awake. Because, like... aren't we

It may just be that what we think of as reality is nothing but a dream. Sort of like being in a benign version of *The Matrix*.

Philosophers from all over the world have created stories and metaphors for this "dream world," non-awake state. In the Zen world, we have,

> Once upon a time, I, Chuang Chou, dreamt I was a butterfly, fluttering hither and thither, to all intents and purposes a butterfly. I was conscious only of my happiness as a butterfly, unaware that I was Chou. Soon I awaked, and there I was, veritably myself again. Now I do not know whether I was then a man dreaming I was a butterfly, or whether I am now a butterfly, dreaming I am a man.

Here's a passage from my book, *Half Asleep in the Buddha Hall* that describes a couple of different theories regarding the fluidity and "unreality" of what people think of as awake:

> Francis Harold Cook describes the metaphor of Indra's Net from the perspective of the Huayan School, in the book *Hua-Yen Buddhism: The Jewel Net of Indra*:
>
> "Far away in the heavenly abode of the great god *Indra*, there is a wonderful net which has been hung by some cunning artificer in such a manner that it stretches out infinitely in all directions.
>
> In accordance with the extravagant tastes of deities, the artificer has hung a single glittering jewel in each "eye" of the net, and since the net itself is infinite in dimension, the jewels are infinite in number. There hang the jewels, glittering like stars of the first magnitude, a wonderful sight to behold.

If we now arbitrarily select one of these jewels for inspection and look closely at it, we will discover that in its polished surface there are reflected all the other jewels in the net, infinite in number.

Not only that but each of the jewels reflected in this one jewel is also reflecting all the other jewels so that there is an infinite reflecting process occurring."

(I am about to play fast and loose with this story—because traditionally Indra's Net is 'really' about interconnection. Or is it?)

As I look into one jewel—'*my* jewel'—I believe that it, and it alone, is the 'real' jewel. I assume that all of the stuff I see reflected in my jewel is the one and only, infinite reality. I also assume that my jewel contains everything else, and therefore that there is only one perspective. Mine.

This is similar to the story presented in ***Plato's Cave***.

Imagine prisoners, who have been chained since their childhood deep inside a cave: not only are their limbs immobilised by the chains; their heads are chained in one direction as well so that their gaze is fixed on a wall.

Behind the prisoners is an enormous fire, and between the fire and the prisoners is a raised walkway, along which puppets of various animals, plants, and other things are moved along. The puppets cast shadows on the wall, and the prisoners watch these shadows. When one of the puppet-carriers speaks, an echo against the wall causes the prisoners to believe that the words come from the shadows.

The prisoners engage in what appears to us to be a game: naming the shapes as they come by. This, however, is the only reality that they know, even though they are seeing merely shadows of images. They are thus conditioned to judge the quality of one another by their skill in quickly naming the shapes, and dislike those who play poorly.

Suppose a prisoner is released and compelled to stand up and turn around. At that moment, his eyes will be blinded by the sunlight coming into the cave from its entrance, and the shapes passing by will appear less real than their shadows...

Once enlightened, so to speak, the freed prisoner would not want to return to the cave to free "his fellow bondsmen," but would be compelled to do so. Another problem lies in the other prisoners not wanting to be freed: descending back into the cave would require that the freed prisoner's eyes adjust again, and for a time, he would be one of the ones identifying shapes on the wall. His eyes would be swamped by the darkness, and would take time to become acclimated. Therefore, he would not be able to identify the shapes on the wall as well as the other prisoners, making it seem as if his being taken to the surface completely ruined his eyesight. [*The Republic* bk. VII, 516b-c; trans. Paul Shorey]

...At the fundamental stage, each person is enmeshed in Indra's Net. Each looks straight ahead at their jewel, and it appears that it is the only reality, containing everything and everyone. Therefore, the other jewels and 'jewel lookers' reflected in an individual jewel seem to be a part of one system.

Lacking another perspective, what we see is what we believe.

It is the same thing for the people in *Plato's Cave*. They thought the moving reflections on the wall were both 'true' and the 'real,' external universe. One man goes out of the cave and sees what's out there. Excitedly, he rushes back inside and says, "This shadow play on the wall is not real, but rather a pale reflection of what is outside this cave." He is heard, but not believed—he's judged delusional, because what he describes would obviate the 'shadow universe' right in front of the cave dwellers. The inhabitants are not ready for this paradigm shift, so they go back to staring at the shadows on the wall.

As individuals, we have no way of knowing what others see, although 'fundamental' social convention dictates that we pretend that we do. Example: does 'love' mean the same to a monk, a spouse, and a spouse-beater? Of course not.

The only way to see the true nature of Indra's Net is to step back from it, thus seeing all of it. Since by definition it stretches infinitely in all directions, it seems impossible to escape its strands.

The release from the Net happens when you move your focus.

Picture a vast Net. It has infinite strands, which meet and join where the strings cross. These meeting-places are also infinite. At each meeting-place, there is one jewel.

Thus, there are infinite threads, infinite meeting-places, and infinite jewels, extending infinitely.

Got it? OK. Now, each jewel contains *a reflection of the entire net, stretching infinitely.*

If you picture yourself staring into a single jewel, which we'll call "your jewel," at your place in the Net, it seems that what you are seeing reflected in the jewel's face is all there is. Right in front of your eyes is one jewel (which is your 'reality',) and it is 'obvious' (to you!) that your jewel seems to contain everything and everyone.

Now, imagine looking away from what is right in front of you. You now directly experience countless others, staring into their jewels. They do not notice you staring, because the beauty of the infinite Net they see reflected in their jewel transfixes them (as it transfixed you before you looked away!) You realise, with a jolt, that they think that their jewel contains everything, including you! How can this be? You know that your jewel is the 'right' jewel, containing them!

You begin to doubt. Perhaps there is more to this than meets the eye! Your first doubt is that everyone 'sees' (believes) the same thing. Second, you begin to question whether you and you alone, possess the truth, the 'real' jewel. You are suddenly aware of infinite perspectives, views, choices, and realities.

You ask, "So which infinite is the real infinite, or does each infinite contain all of the other infinites? And yet, one jewel containing all of the infinites is still one jewel of an infinite number. What if all views, and none, are true? What if all that each jewel is, is part of a larger thing, which I cannot see until I stop staring into my own jewel?

Head numb yet?

This is a mind experiment you can use to evaluate the 'fundamentalist' reality, in which each thinks their rules, their jewel, and their perspective, is 'true.' Religions play this game all the time: 'My guy is the right guy, and your guy is a false prophet!"

Fundamentalists believe that their worldview is 'infinite, exclusive, and correct.' You know this because fundamentalists of any stripe are so willing to try to stuff their beliefs down other people's throats. They puzzle themselves over the inability of others to see things their way. Some are actually more than willing to kill an unbeliever.

At the same time, the 'others' that they are trying to cram their views into cannot see anything other than the jewel they are staring into. They will not change because their own jewel, to them, is 'true,' and yours is 'false.' And they puzzle themselves over your inability to see things their way. They are more than willing to kill you... an unbeliever.

Until you step back. And see the Net. And see the jewels and the infinite possibilities. Then, you begin to grasp that your view is simply a view of a small segment of the whole.

Once you 'get' this, you understand the futility of trying to force others to see it your way. And that is wisdom. Therefore, you stop trying! You see that your only task is to turn your head, open your eyes, and see! Once you see the bigger picture, you can choose to be 'at one' (present) with that which underlies everything, including the Net. This is 'waking up,'—this is Peck's Mysticism stage.

Warning: you know you are back to being caught in the Net every time you think or say, "But why can't they see it? It is so obvious! I am only pointing out their errors because I'm evolved!" You un-catch yourself by living your understanding, rather than delivering a lecture.

Step back and see the Net, as well as what creates and underlies the Net. The energy that underlies the Net and the '10,000 things,' (everything in the known and unknown universes) is what the Taoists call (obviously...) Tao.

For now, let me just say this: the ideas captured above cross millennia and philosophies. The idea of "waking up" has been prevalent forever, and the "waking up" is from *illusion*. And the chief illusion is that "I" possess the truth.

About anything. Including myself.

Waking up is coming to this realisation, and at the same time realising that "everyone and everything" is in the same boat. It's all butterfly dreams. This is this, and that is that, and none of it is anything.

Where all of this gets interesting is when we apply this same idea to our *beliefs*.

Our beliefs are convenient fictions, too. This is easily demonstrable. This week, I watched Sarah Palin endorse Donald Trump. Alternating between gagging and laughing, I none-theless understood this:

They both think their version of reality is **true**. The are totally convinced of it. And they think the liberal view is totally **false**. They are totally convinced of it.

Others of a liberal persuasion think the two of them are deluded at best. And they think that the liberal view is **true.**

I'd love to be able to say I am above such judgements, but I'm not. It's not just *them*! It's me, too!

I fall back into Plato's Cave if I do not "get" that all of us are wrong, right, confused, clear—all at the same time. All stories, all the time. There is nothing here worth killing each other over.

Breathe into your stories—see if you can hold them loosely, and with a bit of humour. Then, try the same

thing with someone or something you disagree with. Breathe, and hold these beliefs loosely.

And then, without rancour or judgement, do the only *important* thing. Decide how you will act, how you will be, and see if you can do so without making a religion out of it—not even the religion of no religion!

On Just Sitting

Eastern religions have many techniques for waking up, and the key one is meditation. In a sense, this meditation is purposeless—it's learning to watch, without clamping on.

We spend a lot of time getting ourselves into trouble. One way we do this is by assuming the stuff of life is here for us—personally.

Rather than seeing ourselves as a part of something bigger, we see everything as having been put here for us to play with.

For example, something simple—like meditation—is declared to have a "purpose," and that purpose is, "to be of service to *me*—to change *me*, to make *me* different."

If you want to see examples of this, try Googling "meditation." What you'll find is a myriad of organisations, ways, ideas about, and "reasons" for meditating.

This fits with the decidedly Western notion that everything we do ought to have a purpose or "goal." Which is not to make goals *wrong*. It's to say that the beginning of wisdom is to see that there is something else going on.

We are trained to identify ourselves as being equal to and *only* the story we tell ourselves about ourselves. We could call this *self*-absorption. We tend to see everything through the lens of "me."

Beneath this, unnoticed, is the energy in which we swim.

The Taoists describe this energy as—obviously—Tao; they believe it's the energy field from which "things" (including us!) arise. The energy becomes *manifest*—in other words, it takes form(s)—and the energy also powers the *that which arises*.

In the *Tao te Ching*, the writer uses a cup as an example, noting that the cup (the form) is made useful or functional only because of the space (the Tao, the formless, the empty):

XI (trans. Ted Wrigley)

We fire clay to make a cup,
But we use the empty space in the center
We build walls to make a room,
But we use the empty space they surround
We form a wheel to spin,
But we need the axle hole to use it
The point:
Having something is good only to the extent
That it makes nothingness usable

Boy, do I ever love that last line. Things (us!) are usable only because they give form to the formless.

Here's part of the first section of the *Tao te Ching*:

I (trans. Ted Wrigley)

A path is just a path, a name is just a name
What is, is, without sense or differentiation
And only divides itself into things when we give names

Forget the names of things and you sense fit and flow
Use their names and you see uniqueness, significance
Each perspective is as true as the other.

The assigning of names is a practical and necessary human activity.

The names of things aren't the problem; names allow us to differentiate, to identify. The Tao tells us that names (form) are one side of a coin, and Tao (the underlying stillness) is the other.

No, the problem arises when we begin to assign *categories*: good / bad, for example. Judgements cause us to move away from relating to the thing named, and into our heads, where we play judgement games.

Why meditate?

Without saying that this is the "right" reason to meditate, one might choose to use meditation (the form) to shift gears—to see the underlying nature of being (the formless, the Tao.)

I've mentioned how many different types, and places, and "reasons for" meditation there are; that there are many styles is neither good nor bad. It just is.

Judging one approach or form to be better than another kind of takes us away from the essence of meditating or doing other forms of inner work.

For example, take this little story about *Tai Chi*

For several years Darbella and I studied and enjoyed a family style of *Tai Chi.* Then we moved and decided it was too far to drive to the class.

A while later we found another school near our home, this one an institutionalised brand of *Tai Chi* that shall remain nameless. We learned their short set of moves, which was (of course!) *different* from what we knew (in the order of the moves) and slightly different as to some of the moves themselves.

I found myself occasionally losing a bit of focus, and when I did, I'd sometimes revert to our old style, something that the wife of the guy teaching us annoyed herself over.

One day she stormed up to me and demanded to know what I was doing in 'her' class.

She said that she thought that I was a spy, that I wasn't allowed to teach 'our' style, and concluded with "I'm watching you!"

She had a ton of judgements, and expressed them, loudly.

I found it all a bit weird, as all I was doing was moving my hands a bit differently from what she was used to.

This would be the "good / bad" thing, writ large. She made some rather strange speculations about me and my motives, *based upon my hand positions*, and then clobbered me with them.

Judgements get in the way.

Anyway, let's see how all of this applies to meditation.

Shikantaza

Shikantaza is a Japanese word that is popular in *Soto* Zen (a school of Zen.) It roughly translates as "only just precisely sitting." Or, as I put it, "just sitting."

In *Soto* Zen, *just sitting* is equivalent to waking up.

- In other Zen schools, *zazen* (the act of meditating) might be taught using devices or techniques—chanting, counting breaths, doing mudras (hand positions.)
- In Mindfulness meditation classes, goals are stressed, or better, hoped-for outcomes are stressed—things like lower blood pressure, for example. In Mindfulness meditation, meditation is a tool to *get someplace else.*

Techniques are used for a reason.

Many people think that the point of meditation is to *quiet the mind*. And when they discover how difficult that is, well, "I just can't meditate," or "I must be doing something wrong" pops to the fore.

So, some meditation schools came up with techniques to *distract* the mind by giving the mind something to do, like counting breaths, or whatever. They realised that without a *project*, the mind is going to wander, and obsess, and story-tell, and this could lead to a not-so-good experience.

Here's the rub: *wandering* is what the mind does, (it is the nature of mind) so fighting it with techniques is likely doomed to failure.

Shikantaza suggests an alternative, (not "right" or "better," just different) and that is to just sit. And observe... the *nature* of mind.

And mind's nature is *restless*, at least initially. In Buddhism it's called monkey-mind—if you've seen monkeys in the wild, you'll know that they restlessly move from branch to branch, always on the hunt for "*better*" food.

With *shikantaza*, you sit, and you watch your mind be mind.

As you watch you discover that thoughts themselves are like clouds moving across the sky—*unimpeded*, each thought will gently drift across your mind. And like clouds, each thought will be followed by another.

The difficulty arises when we start *thinking* about the thought we are observing—when we *latch on* to (cling to) a thought.

We stop the drift of the thought as we start to tell ourselves a story about the thought.

As we latch on, the story we are telling ourselves *about* the thought takes over. We flesh the story out—playing all the roles, having a dialogue, picking a fight, whatever.

This is monkey-mind.

Next, because we were disciplined as kids for being "bad," the norm is to beat up on ourselves for getting distracted. Then we get to have another internal fight and declare ourselves incapable of sitting quietly. Maybe I should count breaths!

But nothing works, nothing stills the mind, because motion is the *nature* of mind.

So, what to do?

Notice your clinging thoughts, your stories, then just let the thought go. Have a (non-counted) breath, and watch again. And another thought will arise, and this time, maybe you can just watch it drift by.

This is *Shikantaza*. The mind is as it is, and resisting monkey-mind leads nowhere, so if I can just be with *what is*, I can be in the flow. I can touch the *Tao*. The base.

In *glimpses*, we see what is in there, in that dark silence. We see the nothing that makes up all things, and perhaps we can even see it for a second or two. In that second or two, we are awake.

Bringing it out into the world

Meditation is a *tool* for waking up, but it would be a pretty lame one if it only worked while sitting on a cushion.

The other day I was doing some rewiring. My first discovery was that the person who had installed a light had done a dangerous job, and I started off on both an internal and external rant.

After a minute or two, or three, I realised that this was not helpful, so I had a breath, dropped the rant, and took apart the "bad" wiring.

Over the next hour, I found myself focussed on the myriad of wires; connecting, pulling cable, cutting, stripping (the wire, not me.)

Very Zen.

Because I was doing what I was doing, and *only* that. Oh, I was talking with Darbella a bit too, but I was mostly focussed on the necessary patterns of connection.

Zen wiring.

Just sit. Find the time to watch the judgements of your monkey-mind. Breathe. Let it go, just for a minute. Or a second. And see if you can see the stillness that underlies everything.

No thing better, no thing worse. Just see it *all*, and be it all, without needing to hold on to any of it.

On Change and Choice

In the last section, I mentioned the nature of mind, and how it's restlessness cannot be changed. It can, however, be observed gently. Freedom comes from making other choices.

Change and choice are not synonymous. Ben Wong and Jock McKeen, founders of The Haven, talked about the two a lot, and Ben would often say, "Change isn't possible, but choice always is."

This is a hard one to swallow, as we've all been conditioned to believe that change is not only possible but essential.

Let's be clear here: we're talking about changing our *internal predispositions*, not something physical. Getting taller as we grew up, for example, is surely a change.

Our personalities are set at a young age, and our proclivities toward compliance / aggression, cheerful / moody, etc. seem to be hard-wired in.

That last one is one I've struggled with.

I describe myself as being *melancholy*; I might "do" happy, but that feeling is fleeting. My "norm" is somewhere right around neutral. And from there, I can and do pulse upward, and can, and have, spiralled downward.

A few weeks ago, I woke up in a blue mood and created a terrible morning for myself. Dar and I were due to head off to Spanish class, and I was sure I couldn't... *couldn't* make it. Darbella, who has seen me in these moods before, said that of course, I could stay home, but that she'd prefer that I go.

I wailed and moaned and gnashed my teeth, and then went. The first hour was torture; I parsed verbs while contemplating deep, dark thoughts.

An hour later, my mood started to lift, and by the end of class, I was ready for pizza.

Now, I'm *not* making light of depression, of which this episode was nothing more than a foretaste. I've been caught in a depression numerous times—one lasted 5 months. I have been down as far as one can go.

I just want to say that my base nature is *melancholy*: my true nature is neutral, to blue, to deeper in the hole, and *I can't change that.* Not with decades of self-work. Can't.

That said, I *chose* to get up, go to class, and interact with Dar and others. I knew that getting up and going *likely* would help me to lift my mood, so I *again* made a choice, a one-off choice, based upon... well... the choices I'd made in the past.

Anyway, many are the folk who get stuck trying to *change*, and what with the impossibility of that, they get caught in a cycle of planning, trying, failing, and beating up on themselves.

Here's how this goes: they decide to change something, and do indeed shift behaviour. They get better results! They get all happy and proud of themselves!

And then, boom. The old way of doing things returns.

Well, of course, it did. Let's break down what happened. The person:

- identified an aberrant behaviour or belief
- thought up an alternative
- implemented the alternative
- got different results
- liked the new results

Here comes the error.

- thought the issue had been *permanently* fixed (that they'd *changed*.)

Nope. All they did was make another choice and thereby got different results. The flaw is not recognising that this new behaviour must be *consciously* applied, *each time*, **forever**... or until you die, whichever comes first.

Choice is ongoing, while our stupidities are predictable. Yup. Nothing creative about us. All we change is the dance partner and the location. The dumbness is consistent.

That doesn't mean we can't *choose* another path. Nothing is stopping us from choosing. Except us.

Notice how often the things you don't like about yourself are "just there." Notice how easy it is to give in and "do the same old shit," and how often you *wish* you were different.

Then, have a breath, and ask yourself, "What one thing, right now, can I choose to do differently?" Then! Do. It.

Then! Do. It. Again!

It's the Zen of moment-by-moment choice!

Ceilings and The Dynamics of Depression

The Buddha said that "Life is unsatisfactoriness." Because we cling to what we desire, and push away what we abhor, we suffer. He proposed a radical solution: learn to see the games you play, and then choose another path.

Depression is simply a label and not a helpful one. I mentioned depression in the previous section, and decided, given the present state of the world, to expand on the topic.

So, a little medical talk, a bit of autobiography, a slice of Zen—and we'll see where we come out.

Medical

First, let's differentiate between how the brain works and what the drug companies want us to believe.

There was an article some years ago, *Newsweek*, I think, that talked in glowing terms about how science was on the verge of being able to create designer brain drugs. Every problem or illness a brain could have was going to be immediately fixable!!!

A decade later, not so much. Recently, a researcher in Europe examined the drug companies' own depression drug studies (Paxil, Prozac, etc.), and... shocker! Antidepressants are only 2% more effective than placebos! In other words, they don't work.

This is predictable, as much of what is *called* depression is not a brain chemistry issue, but sadness writ large.

Sounds so much more dramatic to be depressed than sad, though.

Studies show that approximately 8% of the population has *significant* brain chemistry issues—enough to need some form of medication. For these relatively few people, drugs might just be the only answer.

Back in my youth, Bipolar Disease was called Manic-Depression. It was treated with lithium. The depressive stage of Bipolar is "*true* depression," and being bipolar is definitely a brain chemistry imbalance.

One friend of my parents was a classic "M-D sufferer." When in his manic stage, he was one of the best life insurance sales guys in the US of A. As the manic phase increased, he'd start behaving erratically, but he'd be so *up* that he'd figure, "I'm cured!" and stop taking his lithium.

He'd bring home strangers, feed them, shoot pool with them. Increasingly weird behaviour, no sleep, etc. Next thing you knew—because, no lithium—his brain chemistry would shift, he'd become suicidal and end up strapped to a gurney in a hospital. Went on like clockwork his entire adult life.

This is the real thing. Not, though, what most people, including me, label depression.

History

Back in 1978, I had a major emotional downturn. I alternated between the bed and a reclining chair for 5 months, barely speaking, barely interacting. Almost non-functional.

In retrospect, I would say that this was not a *true* depression, as in a brain chemistry issue treatable with drugs. I was deeply miserable and sad—but I also am painfully aware of how I cooked up drama to keep myself caught in it for so long.

After 5 months of this, a friend happened by and said that he thought I was just bored and unmotivated. He remembered my saying that I'd previously planned on going to Seminary. I sadly shrugged off his strong suggestion that I go, but exactly one day later I "coincidentally" changed what I could change—my behaviour—my actions. I got out of the chair, made a phone call, signed up, went to Seminary and became a minister. I followed that one up with a degree in Counselling.

I also wrote a free booklet called "The Watcher," which describes my process for dealing with negative thoughts.

It's still free, and available for download.[4]

Back then, I also decided that my baseline personality is "not happy."

A few years back, I read an article by Pema Chodron. She described herself as a "cheerful melancholic." I thought that expression perfectly described me.

I mentioned in the last section that there is *no way* to alter (change) one's baseline "self." How we *are*, (things like mood and temperament, levels of pain tolerance, our place in the introvert / extrovert scale, etc.)—such things are fixed—perhaps at the cellular level.

Yet, this is what brain scientists are attempting to "fix."

We need to stop expecting drug companies to fix us. It is no coincidence that, every time a study for a new "mind altering drug" comes out, the closing paragraph reads, "10-13 sessions of talk therapy are just as effective." Talking things through, getting a handle on the games we play—stunningly effective!

That's the Zen part

It is all about *focus*, as in, what we choose to "look" at.

I quite enjoy the French movie, "*Water Lilies.*" In one scene, the protagonist and her girlfriend are lying in bed, and they're staring at the ceiling.

The protagonist goes off on a "French movie" speech (a French movie *must* have a philosophical dialogue to be *French*,

---

[4] http://www.phoenixcentre.com/free_for_the_asking.htm

after all...) about ceilings, and how "The ceiling is probably the last thing most people see" before they die.

She imagined that 90% of people die staring at the ceiling and that this "last thing you see" is imprinted on the person's retina. "Imagine the number of people with ceilings in their eyes."

What you focus on becomes your reality, plain and simple. And the way we get lost and end up focussing on the "ceiling" is through our story-telling.

So, is depression a "series of stories?" The Zen answer would be, "Yes, and so is everything else that is not "*real.*""

"Real" is what is right in front of you, and sometimes, "real" is sad, heartbroken, angry, shut down. In other words, just what our society tells us we ought not to be.

Here's how it plays out: we feel what we feel, and rather than keep it simple and say, "Boy, I am feeling sad right now," we think we are compelled to explain and *justify* the feeling. So, we invent 'evidence,' in the form of stories, to *support* how we are feeling.

My personal favourite stories are variants of

1) I'm all alone and no one likes me, and
2) I'm a failure, and it's all my fault.

Now, I could tell you a *story* about growing up a favoured only child, and how I was treated as superior to everyone, how I never learned to fail gracefully, etc. But they'd just be stories to support my stories.

In truth, when things don't go my way (my *story* of how things *ought* to go,) I sadden myself and sometimes anger myself. The anger comes out as, "I quit. I'm going to take my marbles and go home." I quickly start into the whole 'poor, unappreciated Wayne' thing. I have been doing this since my teens.

If I let myself, one story builds upon another, and soon I'm recalling other times I've felt hard done by. In 1978, I pushed this dramatic story-telling so far that I ended up spending 5 months in a reclining chair.

These days, I find I'm not interested in any of my stories, at least not for very long

Sure, because my nature is melancholy, I see shades of grey (not the '*50 Shades*' version, either!) where Darbella sees fuchsia.

The standing joke for us as we live in Costa Rica: Dar says, "*Que tal*?" (how are you?) and I usually reply, "*Mas a menos*," (more or less - it means OK-ish) while she is "*Muy bien*!" (great!)

Zen teaches us to simply observe the feelings that arise, the stories we tell, and to let them drift past like clouds. Not easy, which is why meditation is perfect—it helps to get your ass settled down for the show.

You learn to watch without freaking yourself out—without adding another layer of story to defend what you do not want. You begin to *explore* the stories, to dissect them, to see them as simple mental games, and as you see this, you can also choose to let them go.

Yes, choose

Being a sad-sack—a poor, helpless victim—is popular in our culture. And being *depressed* has cachet—better than admitting, "I just decided to make myself miserable and then blame you!"

To admit you are blue, sad, angry, bored, etc. takes courage, as you will face the question, "Why?"

"Because it's my nature" will cause others to, at least, raise their eyebrows. But this is the case. What I feel is what I feel, and has *nothing* to do with the explanation I create to defend it. Feelings, "just are."

I'm not making light of depression... true depression is debilitating. I'm simply stating that most people who are sad are not depressed. I no longer find it helpful to claim depression, even though my *behaviour* looks exactly like classic depression.

Instead of labelling your feelings, have a look at your patterns.

What stories do you tell yourself to make your present situation into a curse? How do you *build upon* what's happening right now, (instead of simply *dealing* with it...) and end up with a life story that leads into a hole? Who do you blame, and what do you gain, by the repetition of this theme?

Explore your options, including accepting that maybe you're just not wired to be "happy." You likely can find solace in *contentment*, while not freaking out that you're often blue.

It's not "about" anything.

Accepting that, you can choose to make better moment-by-moment choices—you can choose to engage fully, instead of running away, blaming, or sitting in a green Naugahyde recliner.

Because while who we are at our cores is fixed, there's always this moment... and choice.

It Is What It is

This little slogan is at the heart of this book. It's also put as "The way it is, is the way it is." This is also the essence of the Tao.

We read this expression, and we say, "Of course!"

We buy into it until something happens that we judge to be "bad" or "wrong." Then, out comes the petulant 4-year-old, pouting, crying, moaning, gnashing. "This isn't fair! This shouldn't be happening to me! I want it to be some other way! Wah, wah, wah."

Back in my early days of counselling, I worked with a client who was beside herself. Her husband was hyper-critical, and no matter what she did, he'd find something wrong. She tried and tried to please him—to get him to treat her "the way she should be treated."

Since that wasn't working, I suggested alternatives. For instance, I suggested that her job was NOT to make her husband happy—it was to live her life and to share it with him.

Except, he wasn't interested in her having a life. He demanded that she do what he wanted her to. And the kicker was, when she did shift her behaviour to match what he *said* he wanted, he'd tell her, "You're still wrong, and now I want you to do this!"

He came in for one session. I positioned the two of them in chairs across from me. Throughout the session, he kept trying to move his chair over to my side. After a couple of tries, I said, "Look. You're a client, not my co-therapist. Knock it off!"

He crossed his arms and glared at me, then said I was a lousy therapist for not fixing his wife. Anyway, he only came that once, and by the next session, miracle of miracles, his little "slidy-chair" routine had convinced my client that he was *never* going to become the loving husband she so badly wanted.

So, she divorced him. A few months passed, and she called and booked another appointment. She told me that she was sad and upset. Why?

Quoth she: "I tried and tried, and divorced him, and now, when we talk (mostly about their kid) he still won't listen to me, and he criticises and judges everything I do!"

Me: "So, you thought divorcing him would smarten him up?" (She nodded, sniffing.) "Here's a flash for you. The way he is, is the way he is. You had a kid with him, so you're stuck dealing with him until your kid grows up. Accept it, and move on."

Accept it, and move on.

Accept it, and move on!

"But... but... I don't wanna!!! It's not fair! I shouldn't have to! (S)he can't treat me this way! I'm not done hurting myself over this!"

Crap.

Accept it, and move on.

Not *condone*. Accept.

The "move on" part fixes the current situation, provided you remember that you'll have to continually apply the 'fix.' Maybe it needs saying: you need to do your life *differently*, or the "bad" situation is going to return—maybe with variations—but it will return.

Accept it, and move on.

Here's the key to all of this: the way it is, is the way it is.

Regardless of your opinion. Regardless of what you think is "fair." Regardless of your preferences. The cosmos doesn't care that you don't like it.

It is as it is.

So, stop dragging your feet, and deal with the situation that exists, right in front of you, as opposed to the one you *wish* existed. Almost always, you do this by letting go.

If you need a sniffle break, have one—I know I do. I need to whine and judge and curse.

But then—and by 'then' I mean 15 minutes, not 25 years—get up, blow your nose, and get real. Look closely at how you got to where you got to (hint: you walked there, due to your choices, and there you were.)

Now, what?

We live in a real world, where things happen. Some things are shitty things, some are great, but it's a crap-shoot out there. No one is exempt from having to deal with *all* of it.

Dealing starts with: Accept it, and move on. Because "the way it is, is the way it is!"

Then, do something differently—things will shift a bit, and become the new reality.

Your contentment is all about you and your next move. This is otherwise known as growing up and being an adult!

Self-Responsibility and Waking Up

Another way of describing all of this is "living a disciplined life." The discipline involves rigourous attention, and a willingness to apply what you learn—each time, every time.

When Darbella and I were in therapy, our therapist called Dar *"The Buddha,"* which is not so far from the mark. She certainly does "get" all of this most of the time, and even more importantly for me, has the patience to put up with me, especially when I struggle.

And of course, I do! This self-responsibility stuff can be a challenge.

For example, when I irritate myself over something, I tend to become "indignant" (which is my pet go-to behaviour when things aren't going the way I think they ought to.)

And I have a very short temper.

Back in the old days, that meant I got angry and yelled. Now, I seethe. See? Big improvement!

This *is* a step in the "right" direction. For many decades, when I was yelling I played the "It's just the way I am" card. Except I wasn't stuck with that behaviour; I was just lazy.

Another excuse for acting idiotically is to blame externals—something or someone—for not making better choices.

Blaming, however, is not helpful. It's just easier than self-responsibility.

It takes a ton of maturity to *continually* choose to wake up and choose differently. To take another path. To use your eyes and ears to figure out what's going on.

Easier, far easier, to pull out old, dysfunctional behaviour, and then apologise for the mess you create.

In the past, this is certainly what I did. I blamed my dumb behaviour choices either on my upbringing, or my genes.

I also blamed it on being short.

A particularly weird story: in 3rd grade, I was very short, and being picked on. The gym teacher, also short, took me aside and said I had to learn to defend myself *with my mouth.* I did. I became great at finding others' weak points and exploiting them. I avoided fights by destroying people from the inside.

When confronted with situations and people I don't like, I still *want* to run my mouth at them. Oh, boy, do I want to. I just don't.

Because being self-responsible is important to me.

So, since 1982, I've bitten my tongue—I don't direct my bile at the people involved. I choose to find more caring and helpful ways to address things. But, as Darbella can attest (because we tell each other about such things,) those choice bits of verbal cruelty still exist *in my mind.*

But *actually* lose it I don't. Because I don't like the 'me' that I become when I do. So, *I stop me.* I don't expect *others* to stop me, nor do I expect others to behave as I want them to, nor do I expect others to make my life easy for me.

I stop **me**.

This is what self-responsibility looks like. It's a dance... with yourself. A parade... with only you walking. It's a solo act, witnessed by the masses.

It's all about you.

So, go for it! Find your sticking points, and get out the WD40.

What are you waiting for?

Relating — Passion's Power

Intimacy and Passion are hot-button topics. In our usage, they refer to depth and focus, to openness and to revelling in the joy of living. Much better than settling for the 9 to 5 grind!

Intimacy and Passion

How do we find intimacy and passion in our lives? For some, the search for either is fraught with peril—for others, it is a seemingly unattainable goal.

I think that we find intimacy through passionate *interaction* with life and with others.

A partner in this walk is essential because, for us, being in a relationship is about witnessing and mirroring for self-exploration. Thus, I am in relationship to learn about myself and to be myself, while being supportive of my partner's process of self-exploration.

So, what are the practicalities here?

First, about intimacy: each of us needs one or a few intimate friends, with whom we can "play" the intimacy game.

This is such a lame example, but a couple of friends were visiting, and after a swim in the pool, I was lounging around, reading. Their dog had been in the pool. The dog wanders over and shakes, right next to me. My book and I got wet. So, I said a rude thing to the dog and sent her away. Five minutes later, the dog's been back in the pool, and, you guessed it, came right back over, and shook all over me. Dar was vacuuming the pool, and . . . and . . . she laughed!!

Well, I started sulking and went into the house. When Darbella came in later, I said, "I'm really angry that you laughed at me." She replied, "You might want to look at *why you are angering yourself over this.*" That's mirroring.

Now, I decided to choose to be miserable for an hour or so, but I was fully aware of that choice and announced that this was what I was going to do. In other words, I *owned my own* anger.

I don't care what your issue is—it's not about your partner's behaviour. It's always about yours.

The contract Dar and I have is to stay **present** with each other, to **listen** without attempting to change the other, and to **be honest**. That's it. This approach to life means that both of us have chosen to explore the depths of who we are as individuals and to share that exploration with each other.

The piece I want to reiterate is that with self-knowledge comes *choice*, not change. Change implies that, with time and practice, I can totally stop from being a certain way. This, I am afraid, is not possible.

As Jack Kornfield writes,[5] wisdom is being able to be at one with all parts of ourselves, including the weird parts.

> "Like Ram Dass, who became a connoisseur of his own neuroses, we come to know ourselves as we truly are, but without indulgence or self-pity. When we are truly aware of our feelings while not being bound by their energies, we can choose: no matter what the circumstances, we are free to follow our wisdom."

And then there is **passion**.

From a Bodywork perspective, there is a direct parallel between passion for life (located in the lower back) and erotic, sensual, and sexual energy (located in the front pelvic region). Such feelings are real—and must be felt, fully and deeply.

Opening to ecstasy, to passion, to the utter bliss of life is a

---

[5] Jack Kornfield, After the Ecstasy, the Laundry, (New York: Bantam Books, 2000), 213

spiritual discipline involving every cell of our being.

Unfortunately, in our rush to accumulate toys, bigger bank balances or more notches on the bedpost, we miss the one thing all souls crave—depth. Indeed, most people who "count notches" of whatever they measure their "worth" with are lost in a **shallowness** that only partially disappears with the next conquest.

Instead, choose the depth of passion that comes from taking the time to go deeply into yourself, feel your feelings and then stay there, in a decidedly goal-less way. You are as much "your body" as you are your mind and soul—and like everything else, the three "realms" need balance. Passion is engagement with the depth of you, on all levels, without judging or resisting. More than enough work for a lifetime.

Grasping Loosely and Letting Go

Underneath all the wanting and grasping, underneath the need to understand is what we have called "the body of fear." At the root of suffering is a small heart, frightened to be here, afraid to trust the river of change, to let go in this changing world.[6]

I remember an interesting moment with a friend of mine. We were discussing a mutual friend, and she mentioned that the mutual friend was upset about something or other, and was making herself sick over it—she thought that there was a big, deep problem. My friend asked me how I saw the situation. I replied, "Yeah, I do remember her saying something about that, but I didn't really listen, and I don't much care."

---

[6] Pg. 288

My friend had a moment of not liking me. She was incensed at what she saw as my unfeeling and uncaring attitude. I said, "And now you're upsetting yourself over my reaction to a situation that's not about you. I don't care because the situation, while it seems critical, is just 'this week's issue.' Knowing her, next week she'll be miserable about something else."

I was making a choice not to grasp onto and engage in yet another drama.

There's an old joke about this new psychiatrist who rides up in the elevator each morning with an older, practised psychiatrist. At night, they ride down together. For months, the young guy notices that the older psychiatrist seems unruffled, whereas he feels like he's been through the mill. Finally, he speaks up, "How do you look so fresh at night having seen clients all day and heard all of their terrible tales?" The older psychiatrist says, "Who listens?"

OK, I'm being flip here. And yes, I do listen. I'm noted, in fact, for my memory. Many are the times that a client comes in and says something, and I say, "But six months ago you said the opposite." Annoys the heck out of them.

I'm not trying to be smart when I do this. I'm trying to point out the inconsistencies of life, which are due to the passage of time and to external change.

One of the more interesting lessons of life is learning to swim comfortably in a sea of unpredictability. The Greek philosopher Heraclitus reminded us that you can never step into the same river twice. Many people fervently don't want to hear this. Acceptance of this requires doing away with two beliefs:

- the belief that we can control the world by making it stay the same, and
- the belief that we know anything at all.

Living life passionately is a walk into "not knowing." Now, as I've said, we can't change our nature. We always have within us a part of us that wants to pull back into old, non-helpful behaviour. What we *can* change, if we choose to, moment by moment, is whether we pull back *this* time.

This is why I didn't take my friend's distress as being *serious*. I laugh a lot about my dramas, and I work to teach others to laugh at theirs. You see, this person had a pattern of making every situation awful. That's a baseline, non-changeable part of her. What I see, however, and you will too, if you look, is that all *situations* change minute by minute. Something happens, boom, it's awful. Until the next awful thing comes along. Then the first is forgotten, the new thing comes 'front and centre.'

I once said to a client, "So, imagine you're having the worst fight ever with your partner. Huge crisis, deep feelings. Now, Ed McMahon shows up at the door and hands you a cheque for 6 million. How do you feel? What happened to the fight?"

My friend thinks she is forever trapped in a relentlessly awful life. But stepping back, we see a river of experience flowing by. Nothing is "forever." There is simply experience upon experience. Each experience is neutral until she grabs one and "awfulizes" it. She is a master at this. Not once, but repeatedly.

Now, the opposite of this is to simply *be* with each experience as it emerges and to choose what, if anything, to *do* with it. I know people want me to buy into their belief that there is no choice. In truth, there is always a choice. If we choose...

It's not that nothing bad ever happens or that everything is always the same. The question is, what are we willing to notice—to latch on to? Our lack of passion for life, our lack of passion in loving, is about our pre-judgement (prejudice) that we are helpless victims of a cruel and relentlessly awful world. Yet, time, rivers, and experience are nothing but change. As soon as we "simply notice," without grasping onto anything—a person, a thought, a belief, an experience—as soon as we allow for choice to even be possible, voila, shifts are all over the place.

Living a life of "choiceful noticing" is the way out of the

"trap of awfulizing." We then see with softer eyes and a larger heart, and we discover that, far from being predictable or "the same," life is full, rich and "experiential." Life occurs moment by moment, ever-changing and deep, yet without meaning. All you need to do is notice–to simply pay attention.

Passionate Expression

The penultimate Western (ideologically, not geographically) obsession seems to be with "meaning making." I suspect this is a leftover from the 'ego project'—the socialisation and ego boundary building that is the basis of infancy, childhood and adolescence—and its emphasis on objectification, naming, individuation and intellectualising over meanings.

An Eastern approach is *simply noticing*.

To move into *simply noticing* requires our willingness to 'transcend and include' [7]—we accept (include) that we always bring our egos with us, along with our need to make meaning. In other words, we build upon each previous step as opposed to getting stuck there. And this is so with all experience. Each is added, or included, to what came before. We are the sum of our experiences, and we bring our interpretations with us, all the time. The *transcend* part is that we can learn to move past knee-jerk reactions to what we brought along (*included*.)

In my work with clients, the discussion often turns to passion. Certainly, it's an issue of some interest in counselling. Passion also shows up regularly during Bodywork. I've begun

---

[7] This idea is greatly expanded upon by Ken Wilber; this is a lynchpin of his thinking. For more info, go to http://wilber.shambhala.com/

to think of passion as being like *chi.*[8] I think that passion simply "is"—it is devoid of meaning, per se. Like *chi.*

I'm good at meaning making, and yet it has never occurred to me to wonder what I "should" be 'doing with,' nor 'what is the meaning of,' my *chi.* A good question is, "Is my *chi* blocked or flowing freely?"

I ask the same question of my passion. To ask, "Whatever will I do with my passion?" will keep me firmly in my head, and as far away from *feeling* my passion as is possible.

The ego project teaches us to behave. Our tribes have little tolerance for passion. We learn socially acceptable releases—sports, sex, etc.—but are reluctant to fully 'let go,' for fear of 'what might happen next.' Indeed, clients, upon feeling the *chi* and passion flow, (which is the result of the *letting go* of the tightness, accompanied by the release of emotions) will often exclaim, "This is terrific, but what do I do with it?"

The way out of this feeling vs. analysing dilemma is to gently begin to include the idea of being passionate into one's self-definition. As I see myself as being passionate (about whatever or about everything,) my comfort level with my own sense of passion increases.

Be with your passion, and see what emerges: perhaps a poem... or a painting. A dance. Elegant performance at work. A warm embrace. A full-bodied encounter.

I've lost my desire to *know* about passion. It seems enough to simply be in its flow.

---

[8] the circulating life energy that in Chinese philosophy is thought to be inherent in all things; in traditional Chinese medicine the balance of negative and positive forms in the body is believed to be essential for good health

Sex, Love, and the Journey to Compassion

In the previous chapter we had a look at passion. Now let's turn our focus to Sex, Love, and Compassion. This trio is a progression of depth and intimacy; unfortunately, many never get past sex as a method of connecting with others. Here are some ways to shift that!

Sex as Fun

Bhagwan Shree Rajneesh (Osho) pointed to a continuum—one of many—that progresses from sex to love to compassion. What follows is an exploration of this idea.

I amuse myself with the confusion that exists regarding sex, relating and love. Indeed, one of the weirdest things I hear from couples in trouble is, "We yell at each other and have long periods of silence, and I don't like my partner, but at least we've been faithful."

Ignoring the moronic use of "faithful," (being emotionally available seems to me of much more significance than sexual fidelity) it's clear that such comments mean that the couple is still stuck in puberty.

Here are some illustrations of adolescent sexual thinking:

People around my age will remember the Brooke Shields ads for Calvin Klein— "Nothing comes between me and my Calvin's." Brookie was fresh from her prepubescent nudity and deflowering in *Pretty Baby*. People clucked over the sexual innuendo in the tagline, yet they bought Calvin Klein jeans.

Fast forward to 2003 and to November's *Esquire* Magazine. Here we find an article about Britney Spears, who denies being sexual. Here's a quote from the article:

> "COMPARED WITH THE DEPLETION of the ozone layer or the political future of Arnold Schwarzenegger, I concede that the existence of Britney Spears is light-years beyond trivial. But if you're remotely

interested in the cylinders that drive pop culture, it's hard to overestimate her significance. She is not so much a person as she is an idea, and the idea is this: You can want everything, so long as you get nothing. Obviously, Britney is the naughtiest good girl of all time. But what makes her so different from previous incarnations of jail bait purity—Tiffany, Brooke Shields, Annette Funicello, et al.—is her complete unwillingness to recognize that this paradox exists at all."

Within Western culture is a paradox and that paradox is this: people are obsessed with sex while being obsessed with being in denial about being obsessed with sex.

Darbella was having a discussion the other day with two of her grade 8 girls; they're doing a project. One of them decided to talk about boys disrespecting girls. Ultimately, Dar used 'approaches to sex' as an example—that boys will do or say anything to have sex: it doesn't take them long to realise that the best way to get laid is to profess love.

I don't want to suggest that girls are helpless victims, manipulated into sex. Phooey. I have never thought that women were dumb, nor do I believe they don't "get" the game. I'm suggesting that one way of looking at the game is this:

Boys use commitment to get *sex*, and girls use sex to get a *commitment*.

And none of this has anything to do with love or relating.

Sex, as Dar once elegantly put it, is an *activity*, not an indicator. Or, as Osho put it, sex is a seed that can lead to love and to compassion. **Can**. Not **does**.

Dar wrote me an e-mail from school one day, after thinking about a female friend of ours who was confused about sex and relationships. Dar wrote:

Does sex have anything to do with relationships? In a relationship or out of a relationship is sex not just a way to fulfil your own need and enjoy watching another person react to you? Maybe it helps you connect at a deeper level—I don't know—or is it just a way to play and have fun?

> Having sex certainly is not going to make a relationship happen. In [our friend's] situation that you described this morning—I would think that she should choose between wanting a relationship with this guy or having sex with this guy. If sex is what she wants, then she is doing the right thing but should be clear about what she is doing. If it is a relationship that she wants—why is she confusing it with sex when she truly has not learned how to do a relationship with this guy? How can she know that his perspective is not truly about sex if she does not leave that out of it?

The reason sex continues to be considered an indicator of *depth* is because of sexual embarrassment and immaturity. Sex is given "great meaning" because we're afraid to take it casually.

For many people, it's a hard thing to admit out loud to being sexual.

I once worked with a 21-year-old who, some months earlier, had broken up with a guy for having sex with a female friend of his. She'd gotten back together with him, and was engaged to him.

One evening she went to visit a male friend of hers and ended up having sex with him, on a pool table, no less. The next day she decided she had to dump her boyfriend because she was sure that having pool table sex with her friend meant she must love *him* and not her boyfriend. (Confused? She's *living* this stuff.)

I asked her about the obvious: did she not see that she had just done what she'd dumped her boyfriend for (both had sex with a friend)? She looked confused and said "He did it for sex. I did it because I think I must love him." I asked her what was wrong with being horny and doing something about it. She blushed, and repeated her mantra: "It's not about sex, it has to be love."

Her conflict is what we have been describing—she has a hard time admitting to being sexual and acting out of horniness, no trouble at all equating the wet and warm feelings with "true love." She is so trapped in this thinking that she ended a 5-year relationship because she had sex with someone else. Doesn't that strike you as odd?

This is Darbella's point. Sex is sex and needs to be taken out of the 'proof of a meaningful relationship' equation. Having sex with someone is an indicator of *precisely nothing* other than that I am sexually attracted to the other person. Taken by itself, sex certainly is not an indicator of the depth of the relationship, nor of compatibility, nor of much of anything else.

Lying to yourself about the *meaningfulness* of sex is simply a story you tell yourself so you won't make yourself feel "cheap and dirty" about being sexual.

Sex is a seed, and the seed *may* lead to love. Mostly, it leads to horniness and if we are lucky, a roll in the hay. There is nothing magical or mystical about sex, per se. (Which is not to say you can't make sex into a mystical experience—that's what *Tantra* and *Kundalini* work are all about. Neither of these practices, however, require "love" to be in the equation.)

Part of being a grownup is having a *mature* view of sex, of being sexual and of sexuality. This mature view accepts our sexual nature as both real and "passing." Sexual attraction shifts, de-intensifies. This shifting is normal. A shift in sexual attraction says nothing about the *quality* of the relationship. A mind-blowing orgasm is all about your willingness to let go; it says nothing about the depth of the relationship.

As an exercise, have a look at what you make out of sex—what stories you tell yourself about it—and wonder if the stories are helpful. Then have a moment or two of seeing sex in and of itself. Understand that sexual attraction is a minor and immature indicator of "love," and virtually no indicator of the depth of the relationship. Once you do this, you'll accept your sexuality as a part of who you are. Period.

Love Helps me to Know my Name

Love's Divine, by Seal, from Seal IV

Then the rainstorm came, over me And I felt my spirit break
I had lost all of my belief, you see And realized my mistake
But time threw a prayer to me And all around me became still

I need love, love's divine
Please forgive me, now I see that I've been blind
Give me love, love is what I need to help me know my name

Through the rainstorm came sanctuary And I felt my spirit fly
I had found all of my reality I realize what it takes

'Cause I need love, love's divine
Please forgive me now I see that I've been blind
Give me love, love is what I need to help me know my name

Oh I, don't bend (don't bend), don't break (don't break)
Show me how to live and promise me you won't forsake
'Cause love can help me know my name

Well I try to say there's nothing wrong But inside I felt me lying all along
But the message here was plain to see Believe me

'Cause I need love, love's divine
Please forgive me now I see that I've been blind
Give me love, love is what I need to help me know my name

Oh I, don't bend (don't bend), don't break (don't break)
Show me how to live and promise me you won't forsake
'Cause love can help me know my name

Love can help me know my name.

Let's move from sex to love, as many don't. Or perhaps better put, sex often turns into *romance*, which has absolutely nothing to do with love.

Virtually all love songs and movies with a 'love' theme are actually about *romance*. Now, there's no question that the romance stage feels good. I know a few people who are sex-romance junkies—it's all they do. Little hearts, all pitter-pat. Everything is so perfect. Communication seems to flow effortlessly, and the energy is so chargy. There's this "at last I found my soul mate" undertone.

The shock, the shock when reality dawns—romance is a stage, and it's a mile wide and an inch deep. What blows me away is not that people fall for this—it's that they fall for it *repeatedly*.

Romance is a biological stage that follows the biological stage of sex/lust. This is not to denigrate our biology. It's just to say that biology is **not** *there for our enlightenment*—it's there to get us to breed.

What just flashed into my head, for some odd reason, is Henry VIII. He's the perfect example of the dubious "joys" of the sex/romance stage. The guy was not a fool in the political arena and was even a passable poet. When it came to women, however, lock up your daughters. Talk about being led around by one's 'parts.' Ask Anne Boleyn about losing your head over "love."

There's such a let-down—a sense of disappointment—that often attends the *inevitable* winding down of romance. Or maybe romance stays the same and additional channels of knowledge switch back on. We start focussing on all the things we don't like in our partner. It's not that they weren't there all along. We were just too busy being in romance to notice.

You all know how this goes: we start judging and blaming and thinking we've been lied to.

Our *illusions* about romance—that it is the same as love—are boundless and endless; our *illusions* cause us pain, and still we cling to them. This is why Seal's song is so relevant. I believe Seal has it dead on. He knows that romance isn't love, and he knows what real, true, deep love is all about. He sings:

"Love is what I need to help me know my name."

What an amazing line! But how might a thing called love *help me to know my name*?

Has it not occurred to you that we're here precisely for that... to *know our names*? In other words, to dig to the depths of ourselves and find out who we are, why we are here and what we are called to do?

But if that is so, and I deeply believe it is, why love?

Well, the 'help' love provides is this: *true loving* means that someone cares enough to give me a shake when I go non-present, a shoulder when I ask for one, an ear when I want to be listened to... so that within this realm of "loving permission," I can go deep and self-explore, without getting caught up in the drama of lying to myself.

Seal writes (liner notes):

> "I mean the voice of expression, of communication, how about just being heard? Isn't that what we all want? When it really comes down to it, don't we all wish that we could just be heard so that it would then give us a feeling of validation? Surely this would confirm our existence; after all, none of us wants to come and go into oblivion. We want to be counted isn't that what all the anxiety and frustration's about?"

It's about being *heard* and *known*. Now, I'd never use the word 'validation' to mean *carte blanche* approval. It's more the sense that, having been heard—having been heard no matter how I am—someone actually stays with me.

As I experience this validation and hearing, I can choose to find the courage to be me (to know my name) through rediscovering me. I engage in an endless cycle of going in and reporting back. And Dar does the same.

A small example. Darbella and I didn't start watching the TV show "*8 Simple Rules...*" until after John Ritter died. We watched the 3 episodes filmed preceding his death—as I counsel on Tuesdays at my Port Elgin office, which is 2 hours from home, I'd recorded the "after-John's death episode" so I could watch it when I got home.

Darbella said, "I missed the first 10 minutes. I'll stay up and watch with you." I was transfixed by the episode. Soon, I realised the show was almost over. The last scene, where the kids pile into bed with "mom," was a deeply emotional one. I started to cry.

Dar said, "I decided to stay with you, as I knew you'd cry and you'd need a hug." This is what "being known" looks like—Dar knows me well enough to anticipate my tears. She chose to stay up late with me and to offer me a hug when I needed one. I joyfully made myself safe in her arms.

Seal is also helpful when he sings, "Oh I, don't bend [don't bend], don't break [don't break]"

That's the magic of trusting the "loving process." I realise that my fears of self-revelation are unfounded and that I can be open, honest, and vulnerable—by being open, honest, and vulnerable. I won't bend or break.

I choose a never-ending cycle of love, which leads me to me and back again. Which leads Dar into Dar and back again. As we share and dance in self-revelation, as we learn, ever again, our names.

Choosing Compassion

Compassion might be described as acting in a way that aids and encourages another, without expectation of return.

In *Compassion in Action* [9], Ram Dass wrote:

> "Acting with compassion is not doing good because we think we ought to. It is being drawn to action by heart-felt passion. It is giving ourselves into what we are doing, being present in the moment—no matter how difficult, sad or even boring it feels, no matter how much it demands. It is acting from our deepest understanding of what life is, listening intently for the skillful means in each situation, and not compromising the truth. It is working with others in a selfless way, in a spirit of mutual respect."

The game, in a sense, begins when we move from being the actor to being the action. This is subtle stuff. Let's look at how this plays out in on our continuum from sex to love to compassion.

Sex: One thing we think we'll get out of being in a relationship is a predictable source and supply for sex. There's often a kind of expectation that "I'm going to be *serviced*, and on my schedule." There's also an expectation that if we "love" each other, the sex will get "better and better." Reality, ageing and boredom certainly change our minds about this. Thus, if the relationship only exists at the physical level, we're soon in for a rude awakening.

Love: I wrote about love as a tool for self-exploration, or, as Seal puts it, for "learning my name." This process is '*self*-centric'—the person I am relating with acts as a mirror and a sounding board for my self-knowing, and vice versa. This kind of relating is scary, as there is nothing more fear-producing than revealing what one unearths during self-exploration. It's why some people change their relationships as often as their underwear. They cry, "You just don't understand me!" when

---

[9] Ram Dass & Mirabai Bush, *Compassion in Action*, (New York: Bell Tower, 1992), 4

they mean, "The last thing I want is to be *seen* and understood." "You just don't understand me!" is saying, "Boy, am I ever doing a good job of hiding by baffling you with my drama!"

Being in a deep and loving relationship[10] means that I choose to hear my partner as she reflects on how I am confusing myself. The idea of using love to "know my name" is about noticing all of the times I create drama in order to *avoid* seeing myself as I really am, and choosing to look and reveal "me" anyway.

Now, we turn to compassion.

Compassion moves everything to the next level by taking the other person into full, equal, thoughtful consideration—by being of service to them in their quest for self-knowing.

Compassion turns the mirror *away* from my ego identity—my "Wayne-ness"—it's doing away with the mirror because "it's not about me because there is no me"—and therefore there is nothing to reflect. Rather than seeing myself as "the helper," I simply help. Rather than being "the important and famous actor in my own drama," I simply act. I am there for others, not to manipulate them into thanking me or forcing them to do something for me, but because, in this moment, I chose to be present through service to another.

Compassion, then, is simple and appropriate presence, without desire.

Or, put another way, compassion is the choice to be present—to be in the moment that is—without attempting to control either the *situation* or the *other person.* It's not putting others ahead of me, because "I" am not there. Nor is it about the outcome, if by that I mean "forcing my outcome upon another or the situation." It's about being at one with the process, and through compassion, seeing the other person as being

---

[10] In my book *The. Best. Relationship. Ever.* I call this Elegant, Intimate Relating. See http://www.phoenixcentrepress.com/.

essentially whole. Compassion is thus a verb: compassionate *serving.*

This kind of compassion is likely somewhat out of reach for many of us. Perhaps, though, it is a drink you might choose to sip at. I sit well with the thought that I can repeatedly choose to let go of my ego needs and my need to be special and noticed, and simply act compassionately.

The progression from sex to love to compassion is first body-based, then self-centered, then other-inclusive. I must *find* me before I can *let go* of me, and then be with others without manipulation.

Being of compassionate service, then, is simple and conscious participation in This Endless Moment.

A Summary

As I think about what I believe regarding personal development, or self-knowing, or enlightenment, or whatever you want to call it, I keep coming back to Ben & Jock's "Train Station Story" in "*The NEW Manual for Life.*"[11] The point of the story is two-fold. First, the *destination* of all the trains is the same—death. Second, given the destination, it's stupid to stand around in the train station, waiting for the "right" train.

Many, many people (me too, sometimes) have their lives on hold, waiting for the clouds to clear and for their "special" path to become clear to them. And I must say, while each person's path is *unique* (as in "only that person can walk it,") no path is *special.* There are only two *states*—you're either standing around waiting or riding on the train. You're either:

---

[11] Bennet Wong & Jock McKeen, *The NEW Manual for Life*, (Gabriola Island, B.C.:PD Publishing, 1998), 7f.

Disengaged or engaged.

Turned off or turned on.

And interestingly, in each pair:

The solution to the former is to do the latter–yet we refuse to believe it because it seems altogether too simple.

A friend complained that she was emotionally dead. We talked about her choices, did a little Bodywork, and while she was on the table her eyes popped open and she said, "I'm going to make a new plan and give it to my husband. I'm so excited!" (As an aside, she got annoyed because she judged that I wasn't excited enough—about her imaginary, not-yet-created plan!)

Anyway, in just an hour or so, her whole life changed!!!

Well, no, it didn't.

Nothing changed, except in her head.

Actual work (getting on the train) was still required of her, and as it turned out, she never shifted even one iota in her *real* life.

So, what does this story have to do with sex, love and compassion? Everything. There is a *continuum* from sex to love to compassion. To put it another way, developing and maintaining a solid, compassionate relationship requires fortitude, dedication, and a willingness to ride the train.

In a sense, we ride three trains simultaneously. Sex, for example, needs constant nurturing, appropriate to our age, energy and "turned-on-ness." Where I go wrong is to assume that my *sex* life is indicative of the depth of my *love* life, or my level of *compassion.*

Each level builds on the one before it, and yet, each level is independent of the other two.

And thus it is with all of life.

In other words, a relationship is not a contest. It's a journey. Some days it's blue skies, other days it's raining. Whining about the grey days is silly. The path isn't meant to be easy, as there are difficulties in all of life. The key is the willingness to stay actively engaged *no matter what.*

I know a lot of people who consider themselves far up the evolutionary / enlightenment ladder. And yet many of them suck at relationships. I think it's because, at some deep level, they refuse to understand the *work that is involved* in developing and maintaining a top-notch relationship. They figure they are so wise and deep that it should "just happen."

The truth is, anyone can have a great relationship when **nothing is *wrong***. The mark of wisdom is the ability to stick it out and work things through when the walls are crashing in. Hard work, especially for people who think they are wise and all-knowing.

I much prefer the state I find myself in—where I'm not sure I know much of anything, but am committed to the ride and to the 'working through' of the next bump in the road. I'm committed to doing part of my work on my own, and part of it through intimate relationships, primarily with Darbella. That's my *path.* It's easy when there are no issues, and excruciating when there are, and yet, because of my commitment to the process, excruciating does not equal difficult.

The self-reliant person simply shows up, climbs aboard for the ride, and owns the totality of their experience. I am who I am, and my reality is what I continue to create for myself. The stories I tell myself about that reality are just that—stories.

I encourage you to stay the path and dig in deeply—your life is all you have, and pissing it away in anger, boredom, ennui, or confusion is simply pissing it away. There's nothing noble about this. Instead, grab your life with both hands and give it, and you, a shake.

Then, get on the train!

Engaging at the Core — Body Knowing

I decided, with this edition of *This Endless Moment,* to include a bit about Bodywork and working with the body through other means.

Making Contact

Let me preface this by saying that I learned the rudiments of Bodywork back in 1981-83, during my training to be a therapist. Specifically, I learned Breathwork and Bioenergetics. I thought it was the dumbest thing going. I was going to *talk* people well.

After all, back then I lived in my head and thought that was where *all* the action is.

In 1996, my body gave out on me. I had what I'd describe as a *physical* breakdown, and went off to The Haven, as I described in the section on Deconstruction, above. There, I found the missing piece, in the form of Bodywork.

A little Bodywork theory

As children, we learn to *tighten*—to erect rigid walls to keep the scary stuff out and our feelings in. Precious few parents teach their kids how to *constructively* vent their emotions. Mostly, parents want their kids to *stop* their emotions—especially the loud ones. By the time people reach adulthood, their bodies are guarded. They feel empty, cold, and distant from others—in other words, lost and lonely. In most cases, they've gotten there through bad habits.

Many assume that *numb* is just how adults 'are.'

I beg to differ. Our entire being is a resonating field of flowing energy. Letting ourselves be *numb* means that we miss what is *right there.*

Here's a client story.

She was in her mid-50s, and wanted to retire from her profession but was blocking herself with "responsibility" excuses. She was in a relationship but was avoiding physical contact, conversation, dialogue, sex. She said that she *never* felt passion.

Her description of herself: "Numb. From the neck, down."

Which is not to say she was dead from the neck up. Her head was abuzz with criticisms (of self and others) doubts, despair, and anxiety.

One of my goals was to help her to reconnect with and *express* her feelings—and from a place of *expressing and accepting,* to act in her own self-interest. I'd encourage her to act; she'd endlessly list all the reasons that would never happen.

And then we'd do Bodywork.

Usually, when something hurt (and Bodywork does hurt. A lot.) she'd quietly say, "Oh. Ouch-ouch-ouch." And then, she'd *laugh.* I'd ask her to let go and express her feelings, but she resisted and stayed tight.

Here are a few side notes: Bodywork only hurts when you press on locked, blocked areas. The same amount of pressure on a non-locked area simply feels like pressure. Or, it feels "good."

You can get a sense of how we create a blockage by making a biceps muscle—and holding it. For, say, a minute. You'll notice that after a few seconds holding the muscle tight *hurts.*

Now, if you were to *chronically* hold this muscle tight, your body would compensate, and after a while, the area would shift to feeling numb. You would no longer *notice* that the muscle was tight.

Until you tried to straighten your arm. It would take effort, and it would hurt. A lot.

As you begin to do Bodywork on tightened muscles the first awareness is, "Geez, that hurts!" Prior to pushing on it, you would not have been aware of the tightness, because, see above.

We call numb, locked up muscles *blockages*. Blockages happen as a defensive mechanism and have universal meaning. Releasing the blockage releases the underlying *blocked emotion*; the muscle tightened to hold the emotion in.

Anyway, back to the story. One day, instead of a quiet "Oh. Ouch-ouch-ouch," she let fly—much more volume—louder expressions of pain—and then uttered a few four-letter words. Toward the end of the session, as I began to work on one side of her pelvic bone, her legs started shaking. Her eyes popped open. She said, "I feel like really shaking my legs, like moving."

I said, "Move. Do what you need to." For 15 minutes, her legs jumped and her pelvis rocked. As I moved to her other side, she placed her hand on her lower belly and said, "Boy! Do I ever feel it *here*!"

To make a long story short, her body finally decided to override her head and give her a body-based *experience*. She re-discovered the flow of her own energy, and she liked it!

Her emotional expression happened when she allowed herself to open an internal block to what she was feeling. It also happened as she and I met at her "edges."

My client and I had agreed to meet each other in an open, honest, caring, and vulnerable way, which might superficially be called therapy.

Additionally, we'd agreed to meet under the framework of Bodywork. As she relaxed her edges and let down her walls, we met person to person.

Each session with her was different. Each session was "how it is *right now*." Each time the question is: "What experiences do I wish to 'let in,' and what emotions do I choose to 'let out?'

Our level of openness determines what we choose to do, think, and feel.

Giving ourselves permission to make *contact*—whether it be simple physical presence, through dialogue or through physical contact, is the best way to open to and share the things we've formerly blocked.

The marker of self-responsibility is free will and choice.

I can only do what I *choose* to do, and be whom I *choose* to be with. I can blame others, or I can be responsible for my own life. I can be shut down or I can be open. I can make contact or shrivel up into a little ball.

Our bodies demonstrate one flavour of all there is to tell about us. Rigidity of body leads to rigidity of mind, and vice versa. Being locked up and locked in leads to pain, then to numbness (to ignore the pain), and eventually to break down.

Freedom comes as I chose to let go of my need to clamp down, hold down and be down.

Resistance is futile, the Borg say. Resistance to self responsibility and to open contact at your edges is also futile, as it only leads to smallness, tightness, closed-ness, loneliness, alienation, and death—all before you actually die.

Resist not the pull to visit your edges. Engage with others as you open yourself. In this, finally, is release. And you might just end up with a smile on your face.

The Sex Gene

In the West, we teach kids to be embarrassed by their sexual feelings—we persuade them that sexual feelings are somehow "wrong." Undesirable. Uncomfortable.

Then, puberty hits.

Dealing with raging hormones requires re-thinking and re-learning how to relate to our bodies. Things are changing! But our societies want us to shut down even more. "Lock up your daughters / sons!"

So, for most adolescents, body embarrassment and body judgement *grows*, while the bodily *feeling* is: "I want to be touched "there," except I don't—except I do."

Teens are reluctant to overtly challenge tribal and parental rules and judgements, and especially about sexuality. They go along and seethe inside, or they rebel in predictable ways. So, few adults have managed to become "sexual grown-ups," and some never get there at all.

About The Sex Gene

One of my favourite clients spawned that term. She was describing herself, and the line was delivered thusly, with a sigh: "Wayne, I wasn't born with the sex gene." She then told me she didn't enjoy sex or have orgasms. She didn't initiate sex, and found it a burden to "please her husband."

It's all about the story she told herself. Or stories.

When she was a child, her mother had taught her that women shouldn't have pleasurable sexual experiences; that doing so was *wrong*. At puberty, she'd tried a few sexual experiments, and she'd start to get excited. Her well-conditioned head would *immediately* repeat mom's teachings, and she'd judge her feelings to be wrong and bad.

But the feelings were *still there*.

She couldn't get past the "wrong," so she avoided 'chargy' situations. She chose to be a "good girl"—the contradictions between her beliefs and her feelings became so pronounced that she tightened down physically, and stopped feeling "those feelings" altogether.

Because that's how she told the story to herself, that was her "truth." And this shut-down-ness stuck around even after she married.

In therapy, she decided to dig into how she'd shut herself down—as she let go of the old, "sex is wrong" belief her body relaxed and her new story became, "sex could be *fun*."

After some weeks, she said, "You'll be proud of me! I initiated sex 3 times this week, and had orgasms each time!"

I said that I was proud of her for *many* reasons and that she'd obviously acquired a sex gene.

But did she? I later said, "You've always struck me as a highly sexual woman, who *chooses* to turn herself off."

What changed was that my client started "acting as if." Rather than saying "no" to herself, she started saying, "Let's see." Her life turned from a certainty to an experiment.

Despite years of conditioning and practice at shutting herself off at the level of her essential nature, she is as we all are. Whole. And *sexual* is a part of being whole.

My client chose to let go of long-held beliefs and quickly found a lost part of her *self*—her pleasure centre and her sexuality.

She found that she is sexual, asexual, horny, bored, orgasmic and frigid, all at once and all the time. As are we all. We are every possible experience, and none, all the time.

How we *actually* are, beyond our potentiality, is how we *choose* to be. We are what we focus on.

She discovered, again, her sexuality. And in a sense, she was right. It was in her jeans, all along.

A Look at Bodily Relating: Effective Affection

There's no question that men and women, in the main, approach affection (and sex) differently. I think that *any* instinctual, intrinsic behaviour can be unlearned or deemphasized; but if you don't make a conscious effort, the differences turn the Battle of the Sexes into the Battle of Sex.

(Note from Wayne: I've never been of the "Politically Correct" ilk, and never plan to join up. Nonetheless, as I was writing this section, I noticed that I was beginning to get "apologetic" for talking about gender differences. But ignoring the differences between male and female wants and needs leads to unhappiness and dissatisfaction. So let me say, then, that I'm *generalizing* in the following examples. In my clinical experience, this is what happens. I'm not saying, "all women" or "all men," but rather "this is how it appears to me.")

Let's begin with Affection.

As a therapist, I use the word 'affection' to mean *non-sexual* physical contact—I'm talking about affectionate *behaviour.* Feel free to define 'affection' any way you want to—that's how I'm using it here. Affectionate behaviour might include holding hands, hugging, cuddling, massaging, snuggling.

Here is where the first "sex difference" appears. For many women, affection is an end in itself. For many men, affection is a means to an end.

When I ask about affection, couples with problems in this area will say, "There's not much affection in our relationship." The woman will say, with a sigh, "I'd love to just sit and cuddle, but he always thinks it means he's going to get lucky." And he'll reply, "Fat chance of that."

And then I know that there's a battle going on around the way physical intimacy plays out for this couple. Rather than having a whole range of behaviours, it all gets munged together. Here's how weird it can get. Two examples:

1) When couples are having sexual conflicts, there's often a wide difference about who wants what done with which. There's a lot of guessing and groping going on, and neither person is exactly having a good time. Often, the couple has either fallen into a routine of infrequent sex, or no sex. So, I propose some physical intimacy exercises, designed to explore touch, cuddling, sensuality and eroticism. And I say, "I'd like you to work on this for three weeks. During that time, no intercourse, just touch."

Now, remember, this couple is not satisfied with their sex life and is mostly not having sex. Typically, the woman will say, "Thank God! It will be good to slow things down and just make some contact." The guy will say, "What? Three weeks without sex?"

2) A female client decided to use sex as a weapon by refusing to have sex. Then, she changed her approach but was still mad at him. She says to me, "Boy, am I ever showing him! I have sex with him whenever he wants to, but I've stopped having orgasms!" Not sure what she thinks the lesson is here...

Most people have sex issues, *and* intimacy issues, *and* affection issues. We need to get over ourselves in this area.

More on Affectionate Touch

There's something warming and fulfilling about recognising that the human body is one big nerve. *Touch feels good.* And touch comes in more "flavours" than Baskin Robbins Ice Cream.

Problems arise because of our tendency to be *body shy* and "sex attracted/repulsed." Because of our Puritan preoccupation with "good/bad," "right/wrong," many have made the spurious decision that *any* physical contact is either *sexual* or *manipulative.*

As opposed to simply being about touch.

In all *healthy* relationships, there is a willingness to both accept and freely give affectionate touch. To do so, one must be comfortable with *touching for touch's sake.* Thus, touch *may* be a prelude, but it is also and primarily a thing unto itself. It is a way to physically say, "I care about you."

That this isn't often the case is best demonstrated by the way people often ask for affectionate touch. They say, "Let's ***just*** cuddle," as opposed to "Let's cuddle." We gotta get that 'just' in there to be sure nobody gets the "wrong" idea.

The ability to comfortably make physical contact eludes many people; it takes a quite well-attuned individual to choose to have highly developed affectionate relationships.

Because of body embarrassment and a fear of rejection, or out of fear of misinterpretation, many people choose to keep others, even their partners, literally and figuratively at arm's length. Despite their longing for contact at the physical edge of skin to skin, they harden their hearts and rigidify their bodies. And in the process, they feel very lost and very lonely, and typically make that all about how *others* aren't very warm or caring.

On the other hand, to turn to a friend (or several friends!) and ask for a hug, a cuddle, a back rub, a massage, is the beginning of breaking through the tyranny of our body-rejecting cultures. Reaching out with honesty, candour and humour bring rewards on all levels of our being.

Of course, what this requires is the willingness to talk honestly with our friends about what we want and how we want it. Things left unsaid have a way of biting back.

Here's an interesting "hugging" exercise for you.

I use this procedure when anyone is, at some level, hurting and in need of physical contact:

First, find someone to hug. If you are doing the hugging (and are, therefore "the hugger,") pretend that you don't know a thing about giving a hug. (This is the truth, as we never know what someone else wants, but I digress...) Decide if the hug will be standing or sitting. You decide this by asking the person who wants the hug ("the huggee.")

Let's use a sitting hug as an example.

- Hugger, sit down on a couch, or the floor, and be sure that your back is fully supported and that you are sitting on something soft. You want to be comfortable for multiple minutes.
- Now, just sit there and invite the huggee to sit down, either next to you or on your lap, or whatever the huggee wants.
- Ask the huggee to make him / herself comfortable on your lap.
- Huggee, wiggle a bit and find the position that suits what you want.
- Once the position is comfortable *for both of you*, hugger, ask the huggee where (s)he wants you to put your arms and hands. In other words, make no assumptions about anything. Huggee, ask *specifically* for what you want.
- Oh. And make an agreement that it's OK to reposition yourselves as necessary.

After hugging until the huggee is *done*, debrief. How *familiar* did the hug feel? Did it meet the wants of the huggee?

Typically, when we want something, we settle for whatever we get. This exercise helps us to think about what we want and to ask for it. You can then expand this exercise to any physical contact activity.

Find several people to practice this with. Begin to work at getting over thinking that affectionate contact is "inappropriate" when not contained in a primary relationship. As we continue to discuss the physical side of ourselves, and how we make contact, you'll see I'm hoping to convince you to push your growing edges and limits back.

A Look at Bodily Relating: Sensuality

Sensuality is another "flavour" along the path of elegant bodily relating. I probably don't need to say that the distinctions I'm making are quite arbitrary. There are overlaps all over the place. For example, having a cuddle might feel relaxing and affirming of the affection I feel for someone. At another time or with another person, it might feel chargy or erotic. Sensual activities also run the "feeling range" from affectionate contacts to sexual charge. Everything is totally dependent on *you*, *your* mood, and *your* intent.

It has absolutely nothing to do with the mood or intent of your partner.

I define sensuality as "being fully in contact with the pleasures of your senses." When working with clients who need to "get out of their heads and come to their senses," (cf. Fritz Perls) I suggest that they do the following exercise.

Give it a try!

- Sit comfortably. Begin looking around the space you are in. As you look at a door, internally say, "door." Immediately move your head, focus on something, and name it. Do this for a minute or two.

How long was your list? Now, what were you focused on *prior* to doing this? This book, for one thing. What else were you aware of seeing? The truth is, your mind was aware of *virtually everything* in your visual field, but chose to exclude, or *filter out* the "irrelevant" data, leaving you "consciously" aware of only a portion of the available data.

How did your mind decide what was *irrelevant*? Through experience. You've been reading for most of your life. You learned rules. How to sit. How to light the book. What to pay attention to. Your brain, doing you a favour, excludes what you've predetermined isn't important.

- We're not done. Now, listen for a minute or two. What do you hear?

How much had you heard prior to paying attention? Again, the filters were in place. Your ears were hearing all those things (you don't think sound waves aren't there if you're not paying attention to them, do you?) but filtering them out. So you could read.

- More. Use your skin now. How's the temperature? How's your butt? Numb? Can you feel the chair? Check out your clothes from the inside. Can you feel the elastic or belt around your waist? (Oh! How nice! You're reading my book in the nude! What do you FEEL with your skin?)
- And more. What do you smell? How's your mouth taste? (Where's that coffee cup?)
- How do you feel, emotionally, today?

The point is, modern life is so *busy* signal-wise that we've had to restrict our senses to survive. We have become dulled and jaded by the sheer volume of stimuli, to our detriment. The nice part about it, as you just discovered if you did the exercise, is that turning things back on simply requires *paying attention.*

This exercise reminds us of the Zen principle of *simply noticing.* What you'll notice, if you watch yourself and you're "normal," is that you're pretty shut down—living mostly in your head, in a tunnel, in a fog.

Simply noticing is an exercise in *sensory awareness.* You direct yourself to pay attention. You keep bringing yourself back to attention as your mind wanders. Meditators might do this by focusing on one thing, like the breath. This stills the mind chatter, which is our main way of blocking sensory input. If I am thinking and living within my imaginary world, (I call this mental masturbation) I am keeping myself from being a part of the 'real" world. As the preceding exercise demonstrated.

Simply noticing is about being alert, aware and conscious. It's the skill martial artists learn—to pay attention to their surroundings. It's *being in the zone*—focussing on one or more of the senses. To effectively do this, I must challenge my preconceived notions, and give myself permission to feel and recognise (pay attention to) what I am sensing. In doing so, I am pressing some or all my *repression buttons*.

Touch—The first and most obvious way to work on sensuality is through physical contact.

I amaze myself over how few people have had Bodywork or massage. I think that doing some form of Bodywork on a regular basis is key to getting over body shyness.

And, I think it's essential that you stay in your body during the process. All too often, people receiving Bodywork escape into their heads and either *go elsewhere* or *analyse* the feelings as opposed to simply feeling them. By doing the 'head trip' thing, we deprive ourselves of the sensuality of the experience.

Even though traditional massage is designed to **not** be about *pleasurable* feelings, if we are honest, any skin-to-skin contact creates an 'Aah!' sound in most people. It's just how the body reacts to touch. Not good, not bad, but thinking makes it so.

The best book about sensual massage is a reprint of a 60s classic. It's called *The New Sensual Massage*,[12] by Gordon Inkeles. The book was initially a classic because it showed nude people massaging nude people. It's still a classic because of its lucid text and illustrations. (And the newly photographed nude people still look great! ☺) There's a back lift—stretch shown on pgs. 96-97 that is to die for.

---

[12] Gordon Inkeles, The New Sensual Massage, (New York: Bantam, 1992)

I think it essential for our physical and mental well-being that we have multiple channels of hands-on body contact, perhaps through working with a professional Bodyworker and by exchanging massages with friends. Establish parameters, then settle in and let yourself enjoy the feeling.

Similarly, breathing exercises can be quite sensual. We've described Breathing Posture on our website,[13] and I'll simply say that people have reported quite amazing sensations *simply breathing*. Giving yourself permission to feel the flow of breath and the flow of energy in the body leads to some remarkable places.

Other senses:

Sight—really looking can be a fascinating exercise.

We often limit ourselves to ooh-ing and ah-ing over natural splendours while on holidays. There's nothing stopping us, though, from setting up all kinds of daily experiences to fill our eyes.

One of my favourite exercises is people watching. I suggest that everyone do this regularly and that couples do it together, (or separately and report back.) The task is to sit and look at people and notice what you find attractive. Comment on which parts of the bodies you find stimulating. Occasionally, you'll see someone stunning and you'll have an "I'd do him/her right here, right now" reaction. We tend to push this stuff back and deny its existence, but if you let down the blocks and filters, you'll see that you "see," and seeing is a good thing. And, why would we choose to be threatened by what we (or our partner) judge(s) as sensual?

Sound—same idea.

Go to the symphony, then to a rock concert. Listen to recorded music and see which music makes you vibrate. (I still

---

13 http://www.phoenixcentre.com/bodywork/body_language7.htm

give top marks to Alannah Myles' "*Black Velvet.*") Get someone to whisper "sweet nothings" or interesting suggestions in your ear. Then, try the whispering in public, so you must contain your shivers of delight. Place your lips against a partner's neck, and "just hum."

Smell—surround yourself with smells.

Buy flowers. Go to a greenhouse and smell the peaty—flowery smell. A greenhouse full of Easter Lilies is overwhelming, yet good for a minute or two. Smell the air at the beach. Smell a friend's skin while lying on a hot beach. There is definitely something about the warm skin smell. Go to ethnic restaurants and use your nose. A lot. Smell the air, smell the food. Breathe in. Use fragrant oils and aromatherapy blends when you do Bodywork. An aromatherapist friend introduced me to this.

Taste—have a mouth experience.

A friend wrote fondly (perhaps *more* than fondly) about her love of *Rolo*™ candies. She wanted to explore her growing edges and push her limits, so the next time she showed up, I handed her a blindfold, and then sat with her and fed her Rolos, Mandarin Orange slices, kiwi, papaya, and other tasty stuff. Goodness, she had a big smile on her face... I suspect the rest of her liked the experience too.

When Dar and I do this exercise, we increase the variety as well as the intensity of the experience by adding things to rub on, and feathers and silk for bodily sensations. Hot and cold things, too. The blindfold eliminates most people's dominant sense and adds the element of surprise. One's mouth soon explodes. For hints, check out the kitchen scene in the movie, "*9 ½ Weeks*" with Mickey Rourke and Kim Basinger. Amazing what a turn on milk can be.

So, there are some sensual exercises for you to try out.

Wayne C. Allen

A Look at Bodily Relating: Eroticism & Sexuality

The erotic urge is perhaps one of the most unappreciated in Western society. I suspect this comes from our rather schizophrenic attitude toward sex and being sexual / erotic beings.

On the one hand, sex is used to sell everything, and is an ever-present force on TV, in books, magazines, and videos. On the other hand, many seem caught in a state of acute embarrassment regarding their bodies, physical contact and the sexual and erotic nature each of us possesses.

Human development is such that sexual awakening comes before emotional maturity, so sexual turn-ons, arousal, and the fascination with the opposite sex all happen before one can take a step back and have a good look at what's happening.

We then couple this with the "normal" sexual experimentation of typical boys and girls—and back seats, dark porches and "quickies" come to mind. For the clear majority of us, the beginning of our erotic life is at first a "solo job," then a hurried, frenzied moment of making out—groping, shyness, and the *need for speed.*

By the time we're "adults" and have found some measure of privacy for our forays into the erotic-sexual arena, we've also patterned ourselves with the customs of our society, (which often has a 'sex is bad' theme) and with our experiences as teens (which many people never outgrow.)

I find it fascinating how few people are comfortable *talking* about sex—let alone being comfortable with their sexuality. For most, sex becomes something that is *done to* another, as opposed to a method of sharing intimacy and self-revelation. One woman recently told me,

> "My husband describes it as 'the contract.' I'm fighting that idea now, but I guess I accepted it originally. I gave up my career, had the kids. He expects dinner on the table at 5:30, a clean house, well-

scrubbed kids, and me, in bed, whenever he's horny. He figures he brings home the money, and I'm there to provide the services."

Needless to say, this is not overly fulfilling for her, or, ultimately (and especially since she's cut him off sexually) for him.

Sex therapists and counsellors suggest that what people need to do is to learn to slow down and enjoy the erotic charge. Ever goal oriented, Western "lovers" often seem hell bent on setting the land speed record getting to orgasm. Or, we're tied up in knots about 'how many' or 'why none.' Intercourse, for many people, is the only flavour of expression.

What seems to be missing is the willingness to take the time to find deep pleasure in your body.

Lest you think that I'm exaggerating the level of disappointment people feel over their sexual expression, a recent study found that sexual dissatisfaction generally had to do with the emotional disappointment of the partners regarding the way the *total* sexual experience plays out. It's not so much about technique as it is about intangibles like attraction, timing, tenderness and relaxation.

In a sense, we're not bad lovers—we're bad partners.

Communication flaws and boundary issues are responsible for 95% of all marital problems, and this seems to hold true in our sexual lives as well.

You'll notice how much emphasis I place on making time and taking the opportunity for slow physical contact.

Here's an exercise you can try: (devised, if I remember correctly, by Masters and Johnson.)

One partner sits on the bed, back against the headboard, legs spread. Their partner backs into the space between the legs and places "her" back against "his" chest. The "rules" are: this exercise is **not** to lead to intercourse, and the person *in the front* directs all the action. This is a perfect way to help your partner to know how you (the person in front) wants to be touched, and where, and how. The exercise should take 45 minutes or so. Try it!

The other thing I would mention, and glowingly, is erotic massage. This is about using massage and hand to body contact for total arousal.

Check out Body Electric,[14] a San Francisco based organisation that teaches erotic massage for men, for women and for men & women. The men & women's event is called "Celebrating the Body Electric for All Genders," and is a weekend erotic massage workshop. Here's a description:

> "We use conscious breath, nurturing and Taoist erotic massage to help us remember the connection between sexual energy and spirit. In the supportive community of curious adults, we explore feminine and masculine energies within the circle and within each one of us."

What you learn is that eroticism is separate from sexuality. And you learn to have an amazing amount of comfort with your nude body. And the bodies of others.

Rather than attempt to describe all of this here, here's a link to a simplified erotic massage:

http://www.sexuality.org/erotmass.html

The Uses and Abuses of Sex

Let's look at how "oddly" we deal with matters sexual. Oh. And as a little suggestion for you, check out a *Tantra* book or two, or do a web search on *Tantra* and look for the *Yab-Yum* Posture. This is one of those slow, rhythmic things one can do with a friend, which builds internal energy and flow of *chi*,

[14] Body Electric – http://www.thebodyelectricschool.com/

while at the same time helping us to see the depth possible in performing this simple posture.

So, I've been counselling since 1981. It would be difficult to 'count up' clients, given a couple of stints I've had working for agencies. Several hundred, for sure. And as my mind drifts back in time, I can't remember anyone in relationship difficulty who was at the same time having a good sexual experience *with their partner.*

I suppose that shouldn't come as a big surprise, given our misunderstanding about the significance of the sexual urge. If you've read my free booklets, and especially *The List of 50*,[15] you'll remember that, for me, biological urges are "low" on the scale of motivators. As Maslow suggested in his hierarchy of needs, the sexual urge is a "biological imperative" only one step above the survival instinct.

What this means is that the sex drive is *hard-wired* into our beings, likely at the hormonal or chromosomal level. On the other hand, were we simply hard-wired into sex as a means of *procreation*, we'd only have sex to procreate. So, we should add into the mix the idea of sexual attraction and sexual charge.

As time goes by, for most couples, sex decreases in frequency and in pleasure. This happens across the board, no matter how good the relationship. This is because the more we know someone, the harder it is to surprise and excite ourselves. While the intimacy of the relationship might deepen, the sex often times becomes predictable.

In a healthy relationship, this predictability can become an area for exploration. However, in a relationship where the *creative and elegant dialogue* project has not been undertaken, raising the issue of sexual boredom or the wish for creativity

---

[15] http://www.phoenixcentre.com/freebies/list50.htm

is often taken, not as an interesting project, but as one more criticism.

Sex, in this case, shifts from a meeting of two bodies for a pleasurable interlude and a release from the *world* to a battle and a power struggle. Often, sex is used to *manipulate* the other person into *doing* something—sex is given as a reward for good behaviour and is withheld as a punishment for bad behaviour. Of course, the rewarder or punisher is still caught in the loop of trying to change their partner into the person they want them to be—in this case using sex for leverage.

The way out of this dilemma is a radical thought. If you can get to the point of seeing your sexuality as simply a part of your identity, like the colour of your eyes, then you can begin to explore your sexuality openly and honestly. You can move past the place of not wanting to talk about it because it's private or because your partner might take suggestions as criticism.

If you can get to the point of discovering a range of sexual / sensual expression, you will find the ways and means of exploring and enacting this part of yourself, strengthening it and learning more about yourself in the process.

Once sex stops being *special*, it can become deep and full and real.

If you choose to accept yourself as sexual, you can let go of using sex as a weapon or as a tool to manipulate others. You can stop turning yourself off to punish your partner. You can decide about how to express yourself sexually based solely upon yourself, in this moment. And, as you separate sexuality from relationship, you can deal with each in its own way.

Or, you can continue to play games and fight and argue and sulk and manipulate, in an infantile attempt to get others to do what you want them to. You can make yourself numb, then apathetic, then asexual, and finally emotionally dead.

You are not restricted in how you choose to live your

life—at least not by anyone but you. We need to let go, repeatedly, of the ways we manipulate. Perhaps we can enter an age of self-exploration and self-revelation. Perhaps, we can learn to be free. And reach out to others, in their freedom. And meet. And touch. And hold loosely. And, ever again, let go.

Getting On With It

Here are several ideas about getting on with the work outlined in this book. We'll explore methods and talk about working with others on what we consider to be the most important walk of your life.

On Pissing Your Life Away

So, **when** is the right time to start living your life? **What** is required before you begin? **Who** else must cooperate for it to happen? **How** many more books, seminars or attempts will you have to make first? **Where** is the guru or retreat centre you hope to get to some day?

Inertia, entitlement, and ennui—the 3 Horsemen of the Apocalypse. What is going on here?

The excuses for not starting are legion. The pull of the familiar is huge. And we never, ever want to underestimate the blame game. All of this is what we've been on about throughout this book. And despite this, the ringing, soaring, scary truth is, nothing about you or your life will change until you begin to choose other behaviours and ways of being.

And the joke is, you would also be different if you simply accepted yourself and your life and your games and how you relate. If you *accepted* it all, embraced and celebrated it all, you would move far down the path from the places where you are stuck right now.

In fact, that reminds me that **radical acceptance** is the first step in making different choices. As I said in "If It Ain't broke, Don't Fix It" *starting* involves accepting yourself as you are, where you are, and moving from there.

Have a look at the questions at the beginning of this section. I used the "newspaper" questions to illustrate some of the many, many delaying tactics available.

The most common delaying tactic is thinking that something (or someone) must change before I can, and somehow *that* change is out of my control.

You need to let go of this idea. The only place any journey ever began was from where the person was when they began. There is no special place, no special moment. There is simply this direction, a change of heart and mind, then another direction.

Let's say excellent communication is your goal or path. How do you get there? You don't. You just start communicating properly.

Many clients say, "I tried having a civil conversation, then he yelled and I got upset and walked away." I reply, "Wait a minute! Good communication is one sided: you don't need anything *from the other person* to stick to what you say you want to do. All you need is the willingness to *persist.*"

It's what happens when you work with a good therapist: the therapist does not require that you communicate well; you don't have to do anything other than *show up*. You can show up bringing with you any emotion or experience, and the therapist will work with you as you are.

Now, with Darbella, I know a few things she might choose to upset herself over, so I choose to facilitate good communication by not tossing those things out there. On the rare times that I *have* tossed one out, Dar just laughs at me and tells me to get over myself. She *could* bite; she chooses not to. This is another way of saying that she chooses to engage in her side of the conversation, no matter what I am doing.

Excuses are simply delaying tactics, and the delay is in taking responsibility for yourself and your choices.

Because your ego doesn't want to admit that all that's slowing you down is your laziness and unwillingness to start, it generates people, places, and things to blame.

One of the interesting things about being in my 50s (cripes, with the 2016 rewrite, make that 65!) is noticing how quickly my life is going by. On one level, it seems like I was 21 yesterday.

Life crashes along, and time grows short, and we refuse to admit this. And soon, if we are not careful, we are on our deathbeds, wondering where our life went, what we did and didn't do, how we played our hand so miserably.

Because you see, there is no *right* time for anything, except now. And I mean *this* now, *this* moment, as you are reading this. No excuses. No delays. You do not have forever. And a life is too precious to piss away.

Locational Enlightenment

I coined this term some years ago, following what was my "fastest fake cure." I was reminded of it the other day, having received e-mail from a friend. Another friend did a variant of this theme over lunch a few weeks back. It's an interesting if slightly odd notion.

The Myth of Locational Enlightenment

The fastest "fake cure" I ever was a part of happened in 1987. A guy found my name in the phone book and booked a session. During the session, he said that his entire life was hopelessly in the dumper. His wife had left, his kids hated him, he was going to get laid off at work and he was sick. Indeed, if his pickup truck had died and his dog had run away, I'd have been listening to the number one song on "Country Music Jamboree."

I started into my regular song and dance about making choices, mending fences and how he might recreate his life in a more choiceful way. I got a blank stare. I started again, going on about the way our choices and our perspective dictate our outcome. I said, "I'm convinced that change happens when we do something differently."

His head snapped up. He grinned, ear to ear. He said, "I'm cured! I get it! I know what I have to do!"

I was shocked. The transformation was amazing, and only 25 minutes had passed! I smiled right back and said, "So, where do you want to begin?"

He looked puzzled. Then, "No. I need to go home. I'm going to pack my pickup truck (I just knew he had one), and load up the dog (ditto.) I'm heading to Calgary. Once I get there, all my problems will be over!"

Locational Enlightenment. In spades.

I said, "Do me a favour. When you get to Calgary, get the Yellow Pages, open it to "Psychotherapists," and book an appointment for 6 weeks later. That's when your baggage will arrive."

Locational Enlightenment is the idea that "I can do whatever—communicate, 'be me,' be popular, etc. **there**, but not **here**."

This often happens as people return from The Left Coast after an event at The Haven. In fact, it's such a prevalent thought that Ben & Jock both joked about it and discussed dealing with it as their closing comments at Phase III.

After the final circle, they invited us to leave The Haven behind and go home, and once there, to duplicate our Haven experiences *at home.* They said something to the effect that "There's nothing special here. It's not the place. It's how you choose to act while you are here."

While it's fun to be at Haven and to be surrounded by multiple opportunities for grounded, clear communication, it's *not* the location. It's the willingness and intent of the participants. The Haven teaches a skill set; the skills are *practical*, not *locational.*

The other thing said at The Haven, at the end of Phase I, is: "Remember that you are going home from a 25-day programme—you're returning to your former world. You're going home to the "real world," (the one you created) and it's still the way it was."

Most people engage in and are surrounded by dysfunctional relationships and situations—it's a motivator for going to a Phase, seeing a therapist, or reading this book. You can't stand your life, so you vow to change it. And off you go, or on you read. You "get it," and decide you want this new way of being to be *your* way of being.

Then you "get home," and "nothing's changed." Same shit, different day.

Well, of course. You had to read this book or go to The Haven or *do* something, and you probably dragged your feet getting there. The "world" you left isn't going to change because you do. Your old friends, in fact, will likely be *threatened* by you and your new perspective, and try to get you to cut it out. And you'll want to blame them for "making it difficult to stay focused."

Well, phooey.

Get over it. You are seeing things and doing things differently, and they didn't ask to be included. No one is interested in your new path but *you*. All you can do is stay focused and keep living your life in a new way. Just don't expect help, support or encouragement from your old world.

You just may have to find a whole new circle of friends, relatives and partners, because what you had was what you set up to meet your old, dysfunctional needs. If you want the "new" way, you'll need "new" people in your life. The old crew isn't being perverse. They just didn't sign on for the trip *you* took. In fact, they thought you'd signed on, forever, to theirs.

In a sense, Locational Enlightenment is "right," from the perspective that something must 'give.' What's required, however, is living in this new way, not moving to a new

town. You must re-locate your attention from what *was* to what *is*, and focus in on the new path.

Much will be required of you, and lots of former friends will fall by the wayside. You can't make them come with you because the ride is yours, not theirs. You can't wait for them. All you can do is learn, shift and commit to living in a newer way.

Try moving without moving. It's much more self-responsible.

Soft Eyes

Many moons ago Darbella and I saw a live dinner theatre performance of "*The Best Little Whorehouse in Texas*." The theatre was large and well appointed, and the dinner buffet quite generous.

We did, however, have a problem with our seats.

We found ourselves plastered right up against the stage—one edge of our table was touching centre stage. The stage floor height was such that if we looked straight ahead, our heads were just below the actors' foot level. Clearly, our table was an afterthought.

Prior to the show, we were laughing about how one could not get any closer to the action. Then the show started, and being up close and personal was at first interesting, then not so much.

The actors towered over us, and we had to crane our necks to see their faces. This quickly led to stiff necks. But that, really, wasn't the problem. The problem was that we were way, way too *close*. We discovered a lot of things:

- that the wardrobe people repaired rips and tears with whatever fabric and thread was around, whether it matched or not. Mostly, it didn't.
- that the female cast members, who were dressed in fishnet stockings and underwear or baby dolls (they're playing whores, remember), were all wearing ripped, torn fishnet stockings with pantyhose under them—and the pantyhose had runs, and tears. And,
- that none of the blondes in the cast were natural blondes. If you get my meaning... if you catch my drift.

Darbella and I initially snickered at the "crotch-level view," and amazed ourselves at how much *detail* we were seeing. After five minutes, the novelty wore off; all we could see were the rips, the tears, the errant hairs (gee, that rhymed) that razors had missed.

This story perfectly describes "hard eyes"—an over-analytical, close-up view of the world

All too often, clients want to *analyse* each situation in their lives. They demand answers to unanswerable questions. But wanting to *know* "why" is a delaying tactic—it's delaying the process of letting go and moving past.

If you think about it, focus on detail is never comforting, or enlightening, or fun. Focus on detail has no other effect than to point to the next problem, and the next, and the next.

Much like our seats at the theatre

Nothing we did *from those seats* could have changed anything. We made jokes, we rubbed our necks, we looked away. And every time we looked back, we saw *more details*. Razor nicks. Band-Aids. Varicose veins. Bruises. With each new revelation, our attention was drawn away from the enjoyment of the play, and into, "I wonder what we'll see next—I'm sure it will be worse!"

The only way we could have fixed the situation was to get up and move, or get up and leave. In other words, the *only* fix was less detail and more distance.

Here's the funny part about living life. Staying stuck in the middle of a swamp is not *required*—it's optional.

Or,

***"Engagement with life is required.
Drama is optional."***

It gets even more interesting when we do the "hard-eyed" drama bit about something that's not even happening. Some years ago, we were house-sitting and got an e-mail that stated that the family was coming back in three months... or six months, a year, or two years.

This was not what we'd agreed upon before they left.

After learning they'd changed their minds about having a *set* date for their return, we spent sleepless hours concocting scenarios regarding having to move in either December or March, then thinking, "...but what if they don't come back for...years!"

None of our ruminating was being done *with the family*, and it wouldn't have helped if we had, because they were clear that they'd decide when they decided. All we did was chew, make ourselves miserable, and lose sleep. In the real world, *nothing changed.*

Our detail oriented obsessing was nothing more than a game designed to make us miserable.

So, what was our "soft eyes" solution?

Having "soft eyes" meant that we stopped ourselves from focusing on what was out of our control. The next morning, we said, "Hmm. Isn't that interesting? I guess we'll figure out how long we are staying here when we find out how long they'll be away. And if they don't get back to us, we can always leave when we said we would."

We all have a burning desire to hook ourselves into the dramas that continue to emerge, and that keeps us from choosing what to do next.

Further, most of us are *surrounded* by others doing drama, so at the very least we are reminded of drama's dubious attractions. Most of the time, Darbella and I quite quickly extract ourselves from the dramas of others. We stand way, way back, and watch them spin.

We've had acquaintances upset themselves when we have smiled at their dramas and refused to join them in their dance. "If you were my friend, you'd be as upset as I am." Well, no. It's not mine, and I don't want it. Besides, all that would happen if we *did* bite would be that we'd all end up having a huge pity party and nothing would change.

In our own relationship, there is little drama. Having soft eyes allows me to see Darbella clearly, (seems like a contradiction, eh?) whereas too much focus on detail only leads to the endless noticing of *flaws*—metaphoric Band-Aids. Razor nicks. Stray hairs, etc.

This soft eyes approach plays out when I simply notice what Dar is doing, remain *curious* about her life, motivations, stories, and directions, and choose not to *bite* on her dramas. And vice versa—I find that I can extricate myself from my dramas quickly when Dar is simply there, observing and curious.

We see much more of life with soft, non-judgmental eyes

When we *stay present with* each situation without spinning it into a drama, our focus continually turns from explanations, obsessions, and endless rumination to simply *noticing* situations as they pass by.

And they do. Situations are here and gone. It is the mental games that seem to prolong them.

Look at your life, yourself, and others with soft eyes, and a light heart. Drop the drama. Watch life pass, without clinging. It's going to move along anyway. It's better to simply stay present for the ride.

And remember, you can't repair fishnet stockings.

Going Along for the Ride of your Life

"Life requires riders, not explanations."
from the movie "*Waking Life*"

Much of our life is spent firmly in our heads, trying to categorise things—to make sense out of life. Doing that, we are like someone caught in an endless, boring movie. We see it, we hear it, but it doesn't, at some level, involve us. We are observers as opposed to participants. We are explainers and meaning makers as opposed to actively engaged riders.

The way out is letting go of *describing* life—by beginning to *live* it.

I was sitting at my chiropractor's the other day. I love the receptionist. We got to talking about the weather. I said, "I don't understand the weather this year." Then I said, "I actually don't understand anything. And if I understand that I *don't* understand and *can't* understand, then maybe, finally, I understand." She smiled, then laughed, and said, "I think that actually makes sense."

We spend altogether too much time on the colour commentary, and too little time being present for the ride. What is happening right now is "simply happening," and I'm there. I can spend my time meaning-making, or I can spend my time *experiencing* what is happening. I can't do both proficiently at the same time.

Now, guess which one most people pick?

This is not to say that, in my reflective moments, I can't *choose* to meaning-make. I guess we *do* make meaning of everything, naming and labelling and cramming our experiences into boxes. But maybe we can notice this process, slow it down, and simply watch ourselves as we do it.

Our stories, meanings and interpretations are useful building blocks for learning—I don't want to have to re-learn not to touch the glowing coils on top of the stove. Beyond this act of *informing the present with our experience of the past* is the moment-by-moment goal of living life.

Our lives are a chain of experiences, and our egos try desperately to make these experiences into our "true" life story. The scary reality is that there is no story. Or there are millions.

Exercise: Consider your past. Do the following:

- describe your life, using examples of being poorly treated
- now, with examples of being loved
- being rejected
- being accepted
- being sexual
- being turned off
- failing
- succeeding

Now, which version is "*true*?" Which is "your life?" Are they not simply imagined variants of the same story—selections out of your experience, reformulated to fit what I asked you for?

Who are you?

**You are (s)he who had those experiences,
and you are also
how you describe yourself, in this moment,
in *terms* of those experiences.**

Once you get this, you can be gentle with yourself, be present for your experiences, and enjoy the ride, remembering that how you respond to the present moment determines the entire course of your life.

And the next moment. And the next moment.

Or not.

Because each moment is determinative of everything.

And nothing.

In other words, if you don't like where the bus ride is taking you, get off and take a boat.

And if that doesn't cut it, the next train is available.

You are as stuck or as free as you choose to be.

"As the pattern gets more intricate and subtle,
being swept along is no longer enough."
– "*Waking Life*"

This is what it's all about, isn't it? For those who choose to be awake, the depth available to awakened eyes is immense. Although coasting along, (goofing off, returning to sleep) is always an option, the pace and depth of life, which is quickly streaming by, means that "if you snooze, you lose." The richness of the tapestry is there, despite us and our actions and especially despite our *intent* (as opposed to our action.) In the end, what we "get" out of life is directly proportional to the consciousness and presence we put in.

Each moment is ripe with potential, with meaning and with destiny.

Or not. As you choose. Choose well.

Mentors along the Way

No one walks this path alone. Since 1981, when my therapist-in-training experiences began, I've noticed that when I was ready, a teacher appeared. And the same is true for you.

What impresses me most about my teachers is their humanness. None claim nor aspire to perfection. Universally, they are totally honest about their skills, their growing edges and their foibles.

Thus, personal honesty is the first mark of a good mentor.

Another mark is a sense of humour. I've never had a serious mentor. They all are funny, ironic, witty, and usually sarcastic people. In a positive way, they get the joke.

They speak the truth and will tell you, bluntly and directly, when you are off track. No pussyfooting around. I still hear "Cute, but stupid" from Gloria Taylor, my therapist. Others have been even more direct. Far from taking offence, I laugh, blush and own up to it.

The mentoring process is *not* a meeting of equals. It's a teaching relationship, and that means listening to your mentor while not making excuses.

Look around. I've never had to look far to find a mentor. And the people I mentor or teach show up regularly, in the strangest ways.

Listen. Sometimes a word on TV or in passing will open a doorway you could drive a truck through.

Go where you need to go. Do a workshop, take a course, and do it with an open mind. Pick a direction and stick with it.

Surrender. Surrender your need to be right. Get over yourself and commit to self-exploration. The reason you're stuck is that you refuse to surrender your ego and your neediness and your specialness. Surrender, stop arguing for what doesn't work and stop hiding from your self-work.

Get on with it. Now. And let me know how it's going!

How Will You Choose to Live?

You do have all the options in the world. Everything I've talked about is available to *you* if you are willing to commit to it *wholeheartedly*. There are no limits to the possibilities open to us regarding our personal growth. We stop where we stop by "choice," not because we must or are forced to.

There is either being present as a self-responsible, self-actualized human being or drifting through life feeling hard done by. All life choices are variations on these two poles. The key word in "how will you choose to live" is "choose." No one, ever, can make the choice for you, nor can anyone keep you stuck in ways of seeing and being that you reject.

One client hasn't been in for six months. She's friends with another client, and my ex-client told her that she no longer comes in because, "I understand what Wayne is saying, but he actually expects me to live it!" Horrors! Yes, nasty, cruel Wayne expects the people he works with to do something different—to stop goofing around, making excuses—to become self-responsible people.

One wonders: why go to workshops, seminars, courses, or therapy if not start doing things *differently*? You pay all that money so someone new can watch you whine? Brother.

How will you choose to live?

The Silent Centre

I leave you with one more story, ending where we began this book—at the Toronto Zen Centre. We are sitting there— "just sitting"—silently in the silent centre.

I watch my thoughts come and go, attaching to none of them, following my breath. Then, I wonder how long I've been sitting, and I let the thought go. I wonder what's for lunch, and I let the thought go. I wonder how dear, delightful Darbella is doing with the meditation, and I let the thought go.

Again, and again, I return to a pinpoint of silence and let it expand. Breathe. Let it go. Breathe. Let it go.

Just like life. We elegantly engage with life in the same way.

Experience, then let it go. No clinging, no, "I've got to make this last!" Nothing lasts. Including you. There is one moment and one moment, one breath and one breath. Returning to that still, endless centre is the truth of life.

Sitting still and observing, then interacting with life—without trying to "push" life—is the mark of great wisdom.

I can only do what I can do, and what I can do is bring myself under my own control—enacting myself fully and completely.

I can, in short, *show up*. Everything else is simply drama.

On *Staying* Awake—
Thoughts and Suggestions

Ideas for living in *This Endless Moment*

When *This Endless Moment* first came out many of my readers seemed confused or blocked when it came to what we might call, "*maintaining* simple presence."

So, I wrote these exercises to help readers practice, and I turned them into a free download. With this 2016 rewrite, I'm including the exercises here.

One: It's not the Emotion, It's the Interpretation

I see this one all the time, both in clients and in myself. Recently, a client's wife announced she wanted a divorce. He called, we talked. Since the initial conversation and a counselling session, he's called several other times. In each case, he's upset. When I ask for details, it's, "She's going to get her lawyer to send forms." Or whatever. In other words, he's upsetting himself over the *normal* stuff that happens when one is getting divorced.

The issue is that he chooses to obsess, rather than *feel*

What I mean is that he doesn't feel his emotions cleanly. Rather, he uses the arising emotion to trigger a *thought* about an imagined future scenario—and this in turn blocks or represses the feeling.

To illustrate, let's imagine that he feels sad. Rather than going into the sadness by enacting it—crying, whatever—he immediately begins to tell himself stories, like, "I'll still be poor when I'm 60." His forward *awfulizing* leads to blocking the emotion, then to dire, hopeless thoughts—**and *then*** his brain shuts off.

And in this "brainless" state, he makes lousy decisions.

Because most people have all sorts of issues around the simple *expression* of emotions, (especially the so-called "negative" ones) it is quite predictable that rather than simply feeling the feeling, we *head* off into denial or "awfulizing." Blaming. Whatever.

This mind game is impossible to stop—our little minds do love a good drama. But it is simple to learn to first fully experience the emotions, and *then* to do the mind games.

Doing it this way just might mean a lot less obsessing!

→ How to Use this Idea

"**Have** your emotions," to quote Haven founders, Ben Wong and Jock McKeen.

There is nothing we can do about our emotions. We'll be having emotional reactions to life and living until we aren't. Living, that is.

What is optional is the *interpretation*.

So, when you feel yourself going, "I'm so angry *because* she..." – give yourself a shake. Yell (internally, so the cops don't arrest you) "STOP!" Have a breath. Then, simply state the name of the emotion you are feeling. "I am angry."

Bonus points: Then say, "I am angering *myself*."

As you feel the urge to *justify* your emotion, remember that this serves no good purpose. Instead, ask yourself, "What do I need to *do* with this emotion?" Mostly, you'll discover that simply feeling it fully, then breathing while feeling it, and then elegantly *expressing* the emotion, is all that is necessary.

So, if you're sad, cry, if you're angry, pound a pillow, a heavy bag, or your mattress. Enact each emotion in the privacy of your safe place. In this way you will drop you addiction to stories and drama.

Two: Create an "Awake Moments" Journal

When I ask clients to tell me about moments when they were completely tuned into life and to presence, they usually get confused looks on their faces. Then, as I describe what I'm looking for, the light dawns.

Awake, present moments happen for us on a regular basis. We don't notice because they fall outside of our "observational threshold." So, for example, if I think that people ignore me, I'll notice all kinds of examples of being ignored while "missing" all instances when someone *does* notice me.

Here's what I mean by an "awake moment": you go to an art gallery and stop in front of a painting and are completely transfixed by it. You are present with what is right in front of you, and nothing else. That's an "awake moment."

Now, think about this: if you don't *believe* that you have "awake moments," then even though you are *locked* into the zone of the painting, you "somehow" don't notice. Odd, eh? If pressed, we'd say, "Yeah, but *everybody* reacts that way to that painting." Even if that were true, (it isn't) so what?

Presence happens as we become aware—presence is being aware of what you are doing, in this moment. It is about awake-ness and focus, not about being blank and unmindful.

→ How to Use this Idea

Start a journal and take a few minutes during the day, and again at day's end, to jot down examples of when you were really focussed. As you remind yourself of these events you'll likely remember the *feeling* of detached awareness. (By detached awareness, I mean that there was no "good / bad" dichotomy attached to the experience. You and the experience were one.)

Creating a journal is a *first step* in bringing presence and moment-by-moment living into *consciousness*.

Three: Set a Timer

I don't know if the DayTimer Corp. still sells the clever little timer they used to sell, but I loved it. It had little levers for each 30 minutes in a day. You flicked some, and the thing beeped for each "set" lever. The nice part was that you could set a bunch of levers in the morning and the alarms would continue to go off all day.

I'd suggest that clients buy one and carry the timer for a week or so, and set multiple alarms for random times. When the alarm went off, they were to stop and ask themselves where they "were." Were they woolgathering? Daydreaming? Fighting with themselves? Planning and plotting?

Or where they "simply present?" In that case, the alarm "caught them" being present and aware—doing what they were doing, consciously.

→ How to Use this Idea

Find a way to set an alarm—these days, you can download software for your computer, or use your cell phone or tablet, or find a digital timer that vibrates. (Stick one of those in your front pocket—then think of me and smile when it goes off...) Set it to go off several times a day, for several days in a row. When the alarm goes off, ask yourself where you were.

Keep track of your responses.

Four: Have a Slow Talk

Find someone who is also interested in this work. Set aside some regular time to have a "slow talk." Beforehand, declare this to be a "slow talk," as this approach varies from normal conversation.

Procedure: One person talks about their sense of the other person, (set a timer for 10 minutes) and the other person listens.

Here's where it gets interesting. The job of the listener is to listen to what is being said and *also* to monitor their own head and body language. When the speaker stops, the listener reports what the listener is aware of, internally.

This is different from communication because the talker is simply providing "food" for the listener. The *real* game is for the listener to notice how easy it is to get distracted, defensive, angry, bored, etc. And, what's really unusual is that the listener is "required" to *accurately* and *completely* report their internal chatter! Also, report any physical reactions: "I got a bit tight / horny / etc."

→ How to Use this Idea

Typically, conversations go like this: 'a' speaks, and 'b' listens, sort of. What **really** happens is this: as soon as 'a' starts to talk, 'b' begins to compose a response to what 'b' thinks 'a' is talking about. In other words, 'b' starts talking to him/herself. As that happens, listening to 'a' takes a back seat.

As 'b' composes a response, 'b' also starts having emotional responses. "How dare she!" is a common reaction, as is, "I'm misunderstood and unloved." This colours 'b's' response, but is typically not directly discussed.

In this exercise, you (the listener) report where you went and what you did with what you thought 'a' said. Not for support, feedback, or an explanation from 'a.' Just to get it out there. *For this exercise, speaker 'a' does not respond at all.*

Once you have described your internal process aloud, you shift roles: 'b' talks and 'a' does the internal monitoring thing, reporting back to 'b'. (Remember, work all of this out in advance.)

This exercise draws your focus to what goes on between your ears when you are "supposed to" be listening. It's also about teaching you to honestly report your head games to at least one other person.

Five: Learn to Juggle

No, seriously.

I bought one of those juggling books, complete with three bean bags, read the book, and tried it. Disaster. But being me, I assumed that I *could* learn. I decided that I would learn in my sleep. I went to sleep with that goal in mind, and strangely enough, I woke up the next morning, having dreamt about juggling all night, and I started juggling.

Juggling is one of those things that are sort of a whole body experience. Your brain has to be mostly engaged in the process (although it does get to be like driving a car,) and your hands have to keep moving, and thus the experience is pretty immediate.

Bonus: you gain a skill and are now in demand at parties, so you can stop thinking you are a goof.

→ How to Use this Idea

Buy a learn-to-juggle book or get someone to show you how. (Sorry. I'm busy that day. -grin-) Notice all of the things you tell yourself before you begin or as you are learning—how inept and clumsy you are, how this will never happen, etc. Just listen and have a little laugh.

Our internal judgments—they get us every time. This is how we stop ourselves from being full, complete human beings. However, since juggling isn't "important" I suspect you'll be able to get past your "negative" voices, and will learn a lesson about persistence.

You'll discover that anyone with two hands can juggle. You'll learn it when you convince yourself that you can, or better put, "when you convince yourself that you *will*."

Hint: Initially, juggle facing a wall, so the sacks don't sail all over the place. Count catches, so you notice your improvement. When you drop one, just start again, with no criticism.

Six: Eat With Deliberation

I suppose you could pick something else to do with deliberation, but mouths are simple to operate and always available.

Most of us pack food into the pie hole like starvation is imminent, or eat while doing something else. Yet, eating is another opportunity to find time for "presence practice."

Of course, it doesn't matter what you choose as an exercise for "presence practice"—it's only important that you *start.* "Presence practice" is anything that requires focus, patience and commitment.

→ How to Use this Idea

Find something fun to eat, say a Clementine orange. Peel it slowly, watching the juice squirt. Smell the peel and the flesh. Divide the flesh, and then pop one segment into your mouth. Do like mommy suggested—eat it slowly—chew, chew, chew. Taste each bite, savour each drop of juice. Eat the whole orange that way.

Now try this with other foods, then have a conscious *meal.*

Seven: To Get Ahead, Retreat

When I was working on my Masters' Thesis in Counselling, I needed time to myself, to think, read, write and plan. So, every few months I'd take a week off and go "on retreat." Fortunately, there was a Jesuit Seminary nearby, as well as a Passionist Monastery an hour's drive away.

The Jesuits were a slice. They are highly educated, like to talk and debate, *and* they eat breakfast in silence. The Seminary was lovely—the rooms they rent out contain a bed, a dresser and a desk. No phones, TVs, no crap surrounding you. They leave you alone unless you ask for contact. They feed you, and the price is cheap.

Pretty much the same for the Passionists, except their place is small—just a house—I ended up cooking a couple of meals for myself and for them! And I *paid* for the privilege.

You can find the same deal at Zen and Buddhist communities. In all cases, women are welcome, in case you are wondering.

→ How to Use this Idea

Plan some down time to meditate and reflect, with or without "Spiritual Direction."

Find a place that resonates with you, and set up regular retreats.

Eight: Four Hands Are Better than None

As in, get a massage from two persons—four hands, get it???

I hope you get that I think that physical contact—physical touch—is important. Everyone, from kids to seniors, needs to receive it. And yet, most people don't.

We had a wake for my dad just after he died. One woman in attendance was a friend of ours whom we hadn't seen in a decade. She and her husband stayed for dinner. At one point, she said, "You know, the one thing I most remember about you and Dar was the massage you both gave me 10 years ago. I've had other massages since, but none affected me like that one."

→ How to Use this Idea

Ask some friends, and exchange massages. If you MUST go to a professional, at least once get two massage therapists to work on you at once.

Stay in your body for the whole experience (as opposed to going into your head and making yourself uncomfortable.)

Nine: Picture That

I trust you've seen "*American Beauty*" by now. If you haven't, watch it. In fact, watch it *again* even if you have seen it.

In the movie, the daughter's boyfriend is into filming his life. The dancing bag he videoed is, for me, a highlight of the film. The kid says,

> It was one of those days when it's a minute away from snowing and there's this electricity in the air, you can almost hear it. And this bag was, like, dancing with me. Like a little kid begging me to play with it.
>
> For fifteen minutes. And that's the day I knew there was this entire life behind things, and... this incredibly benevolent force, that wanted me to know there was no reason to be afraid, ever.
>
> Video's a poor excuse, I know. But it helps me remember... and I *need* to remember... Sometimes there's so much beauty in the world I feel like I can't take it, like my heart's going to cave in."

→ How to Use this Idea

Pick up a camera and go photograph or film "life." Look for what is right there in front of your nose—the stuff that you've been missing.

Photograph yourself in a mirror (as opposed to the "selfie-cam") and offer to photograph others.

Get out of your head with this exercise. It's not about your skills, or what you look like. It's about seeing and capturing what's *right there*.

Ten: Use Music to Move You

At every place Dar and I regularly "hang out," we listen to, and "mark" stuff with music. Music gets under our skin and into our deep spots... if we let it.

→ How to Use this Idea

Create some playlists of music that moves you—and that you will move to! Listen to favourite songs and see what the song triggers. Some will touch your heart, some will make your pelvis want to move, some will remind you of past experiences, and some will help you to relax.

Make compilation lists based upon the mood generated. Then, you can use the compilations as a means to an end. Immerse yourself in a musical mood.

Eleven: Dance Like Your Life Depends on It

This is sort of a follow-on to the prior suggestion. I've noticed that a lot of people dance reluctantly, if at all. And those who do dance seem... well... a bit constipated or something.

Having great tunes available is one step, but learning to move to the music is not only fun, it's life-saving. It simply takes a willingness to stand up, figure out the beat, and move to it.

Good dancers also know that one's pelvis ought to move freely, as that's where the passion and fun comes from! So, get up with now, and move your pelvis.

Notice that it can move in a circle, (like a hula) side to side (Latin dancing) and forward and back (gettin' jiggy with it.)

→ How to Use this Idea

I mentioned this above, but play Alannah Myles' *Black Velvet.*" This is a song pointed right at the pelvis. Move your pelvis back and forth to the beat, like you're engaging in the horizontal mambo. Keep your feet on the ground; don't stand on your toes.

Let the movement of your pelvis lead and dictate the movement of the rest of your body.

Or, just go dancing with friends and ask the best dancer you know to help you out!

Twelve: Build a Support Team

I picked up a blank list from somewhere—it was of the types of people I 'ought' to have in my life. People like a banker, a doctor, an accountant, a lawyer. And on and on. The idea was to fill in the blanks with the names of actual people and to choose those people based on their competence.

→ How to Use this Idea

Make sure the professionals in your life are people you both *like* and *want to* work with. Many people end up with professionals by accident, and then get into "Oh well, I got 'em and I'm stuck with them." Phooey. Fire the bozos and keep the good ones.

As to the *rest* of your life, who are the members of your 'support team?' We all need them; people to go to for a hug, for kind words and a cup of coffee. People who are glad to provide positive regard, suggestions, and direction—a team of individuals who love you and will walk with you for the long term, no matter where your walk goes.

One person on everyone's list "should" be your principal partner—if you're in a relationship and don't trust your partner enough to have him/her to your list, fix the relationship *now*, or end it.

Thirteen: Silence Sounds Good

Under the 'retreat' suggestion, (# 7), I mentioned that my Jesuit friends ate breakfast in silence. My Buddhist colleagues often have week-long or month-long *silent* retreats.

An hour here, a day there, silence is golden! So, get quiet!

→ How to Use this Idea

Turn off your mouth regularly. Shut up. Be quiet. Zip your lip.

Get it?

Structured silence is especially valuable. Sitting and eating in silence is an amazing thing. You see people, yet you are alone. Which is the actual truth of life, as we are born, live, and die alone.

At Haven, during Phase 1 (one of the month-long programmes) there is a 3-day silence and fast. They suggest (strongly!) that you do not engage at all with others—rather, you keep your eyes down and make no eye contact, in addition to not talking. This is a profound practice—you are left with *yourself*—with your thoughts, your nuttiness and your drama.

You soon learn to listen to your mind-chatter gently and to find pleasure in silence.

Make this happen for you, soon. Google "silent retreat" and see what comes up.

Fourteen: Be Simple Minded

I was at my chiropractor's office recently. You may remember I mentioned the secretary who works there. This visit, she and I had a long talk about how to sell my books. She was totally present with my stories, and her comments and suggestions were bang on.

What I continue to notice about her (well, actually the story I'm telling myself about her) is that she keeps her life pretty simple. She focuses in on the person in front of her, listens, then smiles and responds. Her responses are measured, practical and interesting.

→ How to Use this Idea

Follow her lead: stop the drama. Life, moment by moment, is both simple and good. Simple-mindedness is what we are 'preaching.' Drama is optional. Have a breath, stay present, and see what emerges. After all, what good has all the complexity you create ever brought to your life?

Fifteen: I could have peace instead of this

This line comes from the book, *A Course in Miracles*. It's a reminder of the power of our intention. Peace is a *choice*, as is pain, or drama, or anger or anything else you might choose to focus in on.

It's entirely possible to shift perspective—where there are drama or issues, there is also peace. As you choose.

→ How to Use this Idea

Simple. Memorise the line.

When you notice that you are tying yourself up in knots, remember: when you create drama, trap yourself in it, then choose to *stay there*, there *is no choice*. There's just whining and feeling miserable.

Instead, as soon as you notice where you've "gone," have a big breath, and repeat, "I could have peace instead of this."

What you will notice is that the drama goes background, and in its place is quiet. In that quiet is peace. In that peace is both escape from the drama and limitless opportunity.

Choose peace, instead of drama.

Sixteen: Tiger Walking

Buddhist teachers of all stripes encourage everyone to practice walking meditation. Because slow, purposeful walking is a new practice for most, you may feel as unbalanced as a baby learning to walk. Thich Nhat Hanh says this:

> "Follow your breathing, dwell mindfully on your steps, and soon you will find your balance. Visualize a tiger walking slowly, and you will find that your steps become as majestic as his."

→ How to Use this Idea

Tiger Walking is a *technique*. Each step is a focused one. Step forward onto your heel. Slowly roll the step forward to your toes. Shift your weight, swing the other foot forward, and step onto your heel, rolling to the toes. Slowly, slowly.

Meditate on the step, taking your time with each step. When you find comfort with the step, start looking 6 feet ahead. Don't focus on anything in particular. Just walk and be present in the walking.

If you prefer a video showing you how to do this, I've made one!

http://chilp.it/c89c4f9 very short version

http://chilp.it/8052489 long version with full explanation

Please note! If you left click (or copy that address into your browser) your browser will play the video; it will take several seconds to download.

Seventeen: Let Go of Outside, Embrace Inside

The way to presence is through *subjectivity*. As we've noted in this book, there is no "real" reality, nor is there an "out there." There's just you and your opinions.

Virtually all distress comes from forgetting this.

When we forget, we get into judging, blaming and trying to "fix" that which is out of our control.

And what is out of our control is **everything outside of us**.

→ How to Use this Idea

Make a list of all the situations, people and things out there in the cold, cruel world that make you miserable, and which must change before you can be happy.

Now, burn the list.

Make another list, this one containing ideas and promises (to yourself, naturally) that you are committed to doing—stuff that will impact on your life and on the world. i.e. don't write, "Jeez, the world is polluted." Write, "Here are 10 things I will do to reduce the pollution I create." Don't write, "My *partner* really sucks at communicating." Write, "Here are 5 ways I commit to communicating more clearly and effectively."

In other words, get over yourself, make some commitments, and then... *actually do them.*

Eighteen: Find a Symbol

I used to present this suggestion as a guided meditation during one of my workshops.

Finding, creating or buying a symbolic object you can wear is a *reminder tool*. This is perhaps the most important suggestion in this set.

→ How to Use this Idea

Close your eyes, breathe deeply and relax. Imagine yourself going into a magical store. The store sells necklaces and bracelets with things attached—charms, amulets, stones or designs. Wander through the store, and keep an open mind.

Simply hold the thought, "Soon, a symbol for this stage of my walk will call attention to itself." Expect to see something draw your attention. It could just be floating there or could be attached to a piece of jewellery. It could be on a poster. It will appear.

Make note of the object. Memorise its every detail.

Now, go out and find it. You will be drawn to a *real* store, (I found one of mine, a gold phoenix, while at an Ericksonian Hypnosis Convention in Phoenix, Ariz. (Phoenix. Get it?) I was out looking for it, walked into a jewellery shop, and there it was.)

If, after a week or two, you can't find what you seek, *have it made for you*. I once used this exercise and visualised a cross with a crystal in the centre. I couldn't find what I'd visualised, so I went to a friend who made jewellery. She made it for me.

Wear the symbol for a while. You'll know when you are done with it. When you are, pick another.

Notes from the Edge

We trust you've found benefit from this book. It's certainly been an "easy write." I guess I needed to get this material out.

What's in this section are resources, references and other stuff to look at. Sort of a map at the subway station to nowhere—and everywhere.

The Web

Wayne's Stuff

We invite you to explore our website:

http://www.phoenixcentre.com

Bodywork references are at:

http://www.phoenixcentre.com/bodywork/index.htm

Breathing instructions:

http://www.phoenixcentre.com/bodywork/body_language7.htm

Free booklets Wayne has written:

http://www.phoenixcentre.com/free_for_the_asking.htm

The Haven Stuff

The Haven: http://www.haven.ca

Erotic Massage

Body Electric: http://www.thebodyelectricschool.com/

About Erotic Massage: http://www.sexuality.org/erotmass.html

Wayne C. Allen

Books

Wayne's

Wayne's books are available from The Phoenix Centre Press, or from Amazon.

Made in the USA
Monee, IL
04 November 2026

67377037R00125